TROLLING
ON THE
EDGE

THE STORY OF A NOYO FISHERMAN

by Jeanne Duncan

Cover design by Curtis Leipold, Graphic Communications, Fair Oaks,
California

Book design and maps by Albert A. Doyle

National Library of Canada Cataloguing in Publication Data

Duncan, Jeanne, 1939-
  Trolling on the edge

  ISBN 1-55212-815-6

  1. Robbins, Patrick D. 2. Fishers--California--Noyo Bay--
Biography. I. Title.
SH20.R62D86 2001   639.2'2'092   C2001-910915-6

TRAFFORD

This book was published *on-demand* in cooperation with Trafford Publishing.
On-demand publishing is a unique process and service of making a book available for retail
sale to the public taking advantage of on-demand manufacturing and Internet marketing.
On-demand publishing includes promotions, retail sales, manufacturing, order fulfilment,
accounting and collecting royalties on behalf of the author.

Suite 6E, 2333 Government St., Victoria, B.C. V8T 4P4, CANADA
Phone   250-383-6864   Toll-free   1-888-232-4444 (Canada & US)
Fax   250-383-6804   E-mail   sales@trafford.com
Web site   www.trafford.com   TRAFFORD PUBLISHING IS A DIVISION OF TRAFFORD HOLDINGS LTD.
Trafford Catalogue #01-0215   www.trafford.com/robots/01-0215.html

10   9   8   7   6   5   4   3   2

TROLLING ON THE EDGE
The Story of a Noyo Fisherman

by Jeanne Duncan

Table of Contents

ACKNOWLEDGMENTS

As a person who never leaves the beach, I have to confess that I didn't write this book alone. I owe most of the fishing "insider" content to my brother, Pat, the narrator of the story, who let me coax all this information out of him over the years. We had some long telephone visits getting the book together, which he might not have had patience for if he had known it would take over 20 years for me to get it right. His wife, Vianna Oliver Robbins, helped greatly with dates, details and review. I was also fortunate to know Rudy Salinnen (the "Master Fisherman" in Chapter 3) who gave me some insights into boats and fishing over glasses of Gallo Hearty Burgundy at my mom and dad's kitchen table back when the book was first taking form.

Many others were generous with their time and talents to help make the book better. I want to thank family, friends, and associates for reading drafts and providing comments. The ones from other fishermen were especially valuable: Richard DeHaven, biologist, author, and halibut fisherman out of San Francisco; my nephew, Jeremiah Waller, another Noyo seaman; retired Coast Guardsman, Dave Wheeler; and Lynda Dale Herren, former salmon troller out of Noyo. Thanks to Felton "Mac" Mailes, for major editing, and to Roger Miller, Joseph and Eleanor Gonzalez, and Susan Zoya, for comments; to Mary Jane Dunckhorst for early production help, and to my brother-in-law, Ed Meadlin, for research.

Special thanks to Howard Makela, of Makela Boat Works at Noyo, and his mother, Marcet Makela (Mrs. Fred Makela), for reviewing the details on Makela brothers boats.

Thanks to Curtis Leipold, Graphic Communications, of Fair Oaks, California, for the cover design, and to Albert A. Doyle for inside design and maps. Thanks also to Geoffrey P. Wong, another Trafford author, for introducing me to Trafford Publishing, and to Joti Bryant and Sarah Campbell and other Trafford staff for their help in publishing this book.

FOREWORD

This is a non-fiction account of the life of a small boat fisherman trolling for salmon and albacore out of the little Port of Noyo on the Mendocino coast of California. It was a spare time project, sparked by my desire to understand why someone who could do any other type of work would choose this uncertain and dangerous life. My brother was a member of this small band of commercial fishermen–more cult than profession–so I began to ask him questions and to make notes for this book. That was 25 years ago.

This book is based on my brother, Patrick's, actual experiences during his career of commercial fishing. That doesn't mean that every word is strictly true. Memories fade over 25 years. The distinction between fact and fiction is further blurred because of the wish to protect the privacy of the other fishermen who shared these experiences, but didn't volunteer to tell their stories.

Pat described his experiences to me, revealing very little about the skippers and fellow fishermen who were also involved. I sometimes had to make up characters and details to complete a sketchy story. To protect the privacy of real individuals, I invented nearly all the names of the fishermen and the boats. There are a few exceptions. Real names are used for the following individuals and boats that appear in this book: Pat Robbins, the narrator; Rudy Salinnen, and his boat, Driftwood; the boat St. Jude. The names of businesses at Noyo are real, including Makela Boat Works. The sinking of the Northern Light was public knowledge, so actual names are used in that account.

Pat says that his stories are not unique. There are a few hundred boats at Noyo, and the skippers and fishermen from each one of them have similar stories to tell. Many of them are the shared experiences of all the Noyo fishermen. Every fisherman who reads this book may see himself or one of his colleagues mirrored in some person described in this book. The author had no intention to portray any actual person, except Pat Robbins and Rudy Salinnen, and any such similarities are due solely to the common experiences of fishermen, or to coincidence. My focus was to communicate the experience of fishing on small, wooden boats.

The small, wooden boats you see at Noyo and at other ports from Half Moon Bay to Astoria, were the mainstay of the U.S. fishing industry in the 1960s, when 55 percent of the fish caught in the U.S. was caught on the west coast. The growth of the frozen food industry in the mid-sixties brought higher demand and larger, steel boats. The diminished role of the small boats now is to supply premium fresh fish to local markets and discriminating restaurants. They can continue only because they can fish economically where fish stocks would not support operating larger boats.

On every coast of every continent throughout the world are similar small boats: in China, Japan, every Mediterranean port, and on both U.S. coasts. These colorful little boats are significant in the art, but not the literature, of every country with a coastline. You see paintings featuring the boats, but very little is written about the fishermen who survive with them.

This book is the story of just one of these fishermen. It is my hope that it will give the reader a glimpse of why this life has such a strong appeal for him, as he describes his experiences at sea. The book tells you about the differences between small boats for the east coast and the west; wooden boats vs. steel boats; the intricacies of splitting salmon for lox; details about fishing techniques, and how to avoid the perils. But it also lets you glimpse the exhilaration of living on the edge that the narrator and his colleagues thrive on.

These fishermen are among the last enduring journeymen in the oldest sense (de jour) who earn their daily bread by means of their skill, courage, and a risk they approach on an individual basis. They are David to the ocean's Goliath–and they win most of the time. They lead lives of rare simplicity. Beating the odds every day lets them know they exist in a way most people never feel. The fisherman would never say, "I survive, therefore I am," but his enthusiasm for this hard and dangerous life says it for him. But, as the book reveals, there may be a stronger appeal even than that.

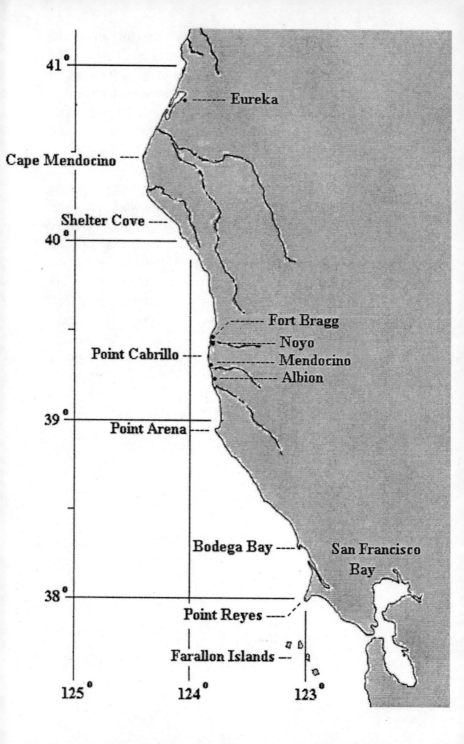

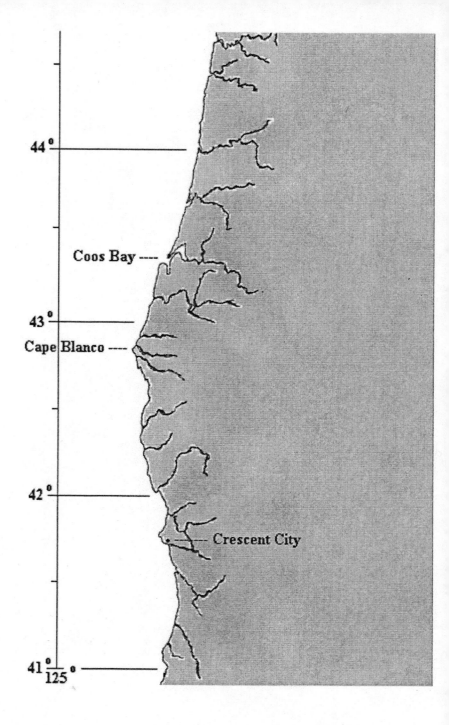

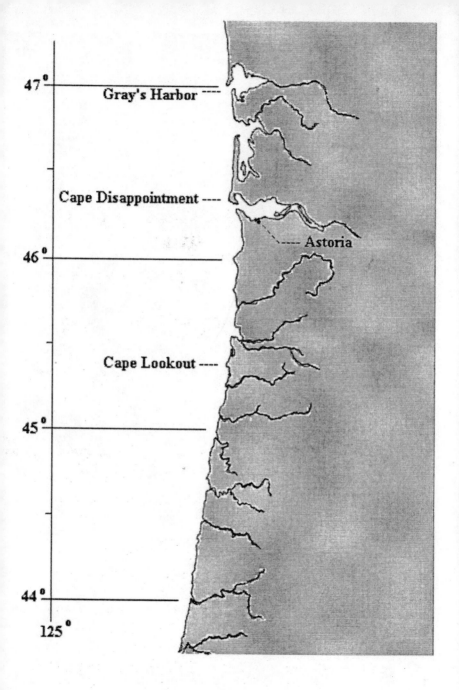

CHAPTER 1

THE MYSTERY

In a way I never felt that my life was my own, because I was a replacement kid. Two years before I was born, my older brother, John Charles, was riding his bicycle and was killed by a drunk driver. He was nine, and his birthday was December 10th. Mine was December 9th, 1948.

My name is Patrick David Robbins, but I got called Johnnie a lot. It confused me when I was little, so they told me about Johnnie's death when I was pretty young. I sort of had the idea that I was him. As I got older I found myself wishing I had known him, so I'd know what I was supposed to be like. Nobody did that intentionally or even realized it, but that was how I started to think.

Having a brother who died so young should probably have made me more cautious, but it seemed to have the opposite effect. I am careful, but danger has never stopped me from doing anything. I was into racing dirt bikes and fast cars in high school, but extreme sports were just games. I found out what an exciting life was really about when I started commercial fishing.

My parents had unlimited ambition for me, but about the only thing that really mattered to them was that I stay safe. I felt that obligation, so there was always pressure on me to do something besides fish for a living. But the ocean has insidious ways of enchanting and compelling certain people, and once you are a true fisherman, it's nearly impossible to give it up for a lesser existence. I struggled with it for a lot of years, and always went back to it.

I finally did break away, motivated by an astonishing chain of events that caused a friend of mine to also leave fishing. At that time, I would not have believed I would ever live on the desert. Certainly, I never expected to find myself at High Desert State Prison, a level 4 top security prison with extremely dangerous inmates, but I have been here or at the nearby Correctional Center in Susanville now for almost twenty years. I still think about fishing every day. I'd be back fishing tomorrow if I could. I can close my eyes, and I'm back at Noyo Harbor.

Noyo Harbor, 1948-1958

Like most of the fishermen here, I began life as a cliff-dweller overlooking the Pacific Ocean north of Mendocino. The ocean's roar has always been the background sound of my world. Its steady pounding against the shore is a second heartbeat I no longer hear, but feel.

If I go inland overnight I get an apprehensive feeling: something is wrong, but I don't know what. Eventually I figure it out. It's the unnatural silence--the absence of the ocean. When I come back I hear the same loud rumble the tourists hear--a constant roar like a loud train or a large airplane. After a few hours I can't hear it anymore. It goes back into the realm of unconscious feeling, and things are back to normal.

When I was three years old I ran in the icy surf until my feet and legs were numb and tingling. There are no unknown terrors lurking there for me. The sea urchins and jellyfish, the undertow and the tide are all familiar hazards. As a small child, I learned to be ever wary of the stealthy wave bigger than the rest, and to know it wouldn't be the ninth wave--or in any other way predictable. I'm attuned to the ocean.

My heroes were always the fishermen. I watched them in their small boats trolling the waters far beyond the beach, and knew that someday I would be out there with them. As I got older, I added another dream I fully expected to realize.

The Mendocino coast has a narrow, winding road, State Highway One, that clings to cliffs high above the ocean, giving dazzling views of the surf below. The roads that connect Highway One with the outside world are equally challenging, creeping through the peaks and valleys of the Coast Range through dense redwood forests. These roads were invented for Formula 1 cars--or the other way around. To navigate them you need something low and built to negotiate curves, like a Ferrari.

At sixteen I had two goals in life. One was to own a Ferrari. The other was to someday own a wooden fishing boat built by the Makela brothers. By the time I was nineteen, I had made good progress toward the Ferrari. I had owned 194 cars, some of them for less than a week, always trading up. I rarely had more than one at a time, so I was the best customer of the local Department of Motor Vehicles office. In fact, the DMV manager once threatened to make me buy a dealer's license if I bought and sold any more vehicles.

They were clunkers at first that didn't even run, and later some that ran but had something seriously wrong with them. I'd scrounge up parts, get help from friends, and eventually I'd get the latest one running. Then I'd sell it and get one a little bit better. I would keep one I liked and drive it around, but it was always for sale at the right price.

Two of my mother's brothers were master mechanics, one diesel and the other gasoline engines, but I never was around them much. I learned the same way they did, out of necessity. They grew up in remote parts of the high desert in Lassen County. My mother told me her "papa" used to bring home car parts, and he expected the boys to put them together and make a car that worked. Uncle Vernon and Uncle Ellis had only the most basic tools, and nothing approaching a machine shop at the one-room schools they attended. Still, they succeeded in getting cars to run, even if they had to modify or make parts.

It was easier for me, because I had friends around who had great workshops, and I also had the Rice family genes. The defining characteristic of my mother's branch of the Rices wasn't mechanical ability, or sheer determination, although they had both. It was the conviction that if you were a Rice, you could do anything you wanted to do, if you wanted it badly enough. All of us have more confidence than we have any logical reason to have.

Even so, my other ambition couldn't be realized with the same simple formula of getting better and better boats until I had the boat of my dreams. First, I couldn't afford even the cheapest fishing boat. Then there was the matter of learning how to fish. You want to learn the various types of fishing from somebody expert before you even think about having your own boat. While you're learning, if you work hard and have some exceptional fishing luck, you might eventually earn enough money to buy your first boat. I'm determined, but I realize this is going to take some time. What I don't know is that, like the Ferrari, when it is within reach, I'll pass it up for something else. But, unlike the Ferrari, not because I want to.

The Silence of the Fishermen

I knew from growing up here that being a fisherman had its dark side, but none of them talk about it. My sister calls it "the silence of the fishermen" and thinks it's some kind of pledge among them. It isn't--it's just a common trait. For one thing, you think nobody would be interested in the routine stuff. But she insists that all commercial fishermen are strangely silent about what it's like out there, and especially about anything that happens to any of them.

When a boat is lost, it's a personal tragedy for every other fisherman in the harbor. And if you ask any one of them what happened to John's, or Bill's, or Tony's boat, he will tell you it went on the rocks off Todd's Point, or whatever it did, usually in about ten words. He will not speculate for you about why, although he probably has some idea.

I'll admit that's true. Just after I started fishing, I remember one boat wreck with a special aura of mystery. The boat capsized just outside the harbor, and a crewman was lost. The skipper was rescued, and nobody ever mentioned anything but the barest facts. It was stormy, but not a bad storm; everybody else made it in. The boat was one of the most seaworthy in the harbor, and the skipper had navigated it successfully for most of his life.

I knew the crewman's best friend, who had been a fisherman but now was operating a dock. I asked him what he thought might have happened. He said, "It went on the rocks."

We were pretty good friends. We talked a while longer, and I told him I was curious about why it was that fishermen would almost never talk about what happened when a boat was lost, even when they knew. "If you fished for a while, you wouldn't talk about it either." He didn't explain, but after thinking a few minutes he said, "Fishermen are very selfish with their lives."

Now that I have fished for a while, I'm the same way. If I didn't see it happen, I'll say, "It went on the rocks," because that's all I know for sure. We might learn from someone else's misfortune, but you won't hear us discussing it. In most cases, it will always be a mystery for me, so I'm not going to reduce it to a simple explanation for somebody else. Fishermen learn to live with uncertainty. It might have more to do with our relationship with the sea than with each other. You know that anything can happen out there.

Noyo Harbor - 1955
Sinking of the Northern Light

Noyo Harbor is in a little cove on the rocky northern California coast, half way between San Francisco and Eureka. It's a harbor by the same standard that the Noyo River is called a river. A stream of that size in the east or midwest would be considered a creek. The natives, surrounded by giant redwood trees, are not given to exaggeration; those little "dog holes" are simply all we have in the way of shelter from a storm, so they serve as harbors. They started calling them "dog holes" when lumber schooners used them in the 1850s, because they are, figuratively, just about big enough for a dog to crawl into. They're cozy and safe when you get in them, but getting in is the trick.

The harbor is settled between high bluffs where the Noyo River runs into the sea. (It's the harbor you know as "Cabot Cove" if you've ever watched "Murder, She Wrote" on TV. The harbor scenes are filmed at Noyo, and the village scenes are Mendocino--actually twelve miles south of Noyo.) There is a backdrop of evergreen hills, and behind them redwood forests. The main highway is on the cliffs above, and a dramatic bridge spans the cliffs to frame the scene as boats go in and out of the harbor.

Visitors consider Noyo picturesque. Sea gulls perch on the creosoted pilings of the docks, and sea lions bark on the rocks across the river. On foggy mornings, tourists like to drink coffee in the warm cafes and watch the boats glide past and out through the channel to the open sea. In the evenings, they like to sip wine or cocktails in dockside restaurants and watch the boats glide in.

It's a calming experience to watch the boats come in at sunset, unless you're a fisherman and know what it takes to get into that harbor. It's always the most exciting part of any fishing trip--no matter what happens out there. It's a narrow, treacherous channel.

Fishermen from other ports avoid Noyo. If they are blown in, they always prefer it's near some other harbor. No one likes an unfamiliar port, but Noyo has a special reputation for being difficult to get into. Its reputation is sometimes exaggerated, but it is deserved.

On a calm day there isn't any real danger, especially at high tide, unless you just come barreling in there. Just about everybody on the river has done that once. Nobody does it more than once.

When you come into the cove on the south side of the buoy and get within about 100 feet of the jetty, you would naturally assume it's clear all the way in. It's not. There is a bad wash rock that sticks right out into the channel. [In about 1962, the U.S. Army Corps of Engineers attempted to remove this rock as a "hazard to navigation". They only succeeded in blowing the top off, so now it can only be seen on a minus tide, which makes it more hazardous than it was before.] It's marked on the charts and the fishermen know it is there. So you get to the second buoy and then head for the north jetty, instead of going straight into the channel. Then, when you get to the tip of the north jetty, you turn south.

This is where it gets tricky. If you turn at too much of an angle, you set yourself broadside to a westerly swell and it's hard to turn with any accuracy. You can get pushed more sideways than you intended. It's not a big problem if you're careful, but you never take it for granted.

The right way to come into Noyo is at a speed just a little bit above an idle, so you have zero to full power for turning if you need it. The rudder on a fishing boat isn't any bigger than it has to be, and it is only effective if the propeller is pushing water past it faster than the whole boat is being pushed. It is not nearly as large as the rudder on a sailboat, nor as effective at low speed.

Even on the calmest day, there is always an anxious moment just inside the jetty. It's only 80 feet wide, and you're taking up some of the width. There are always swells, and the rocks along the jetty are not far away. If it's choppy, they seem even closer than they are. And there's always a chance, if the waves are high, that one coming up behind you could break over the stern and swamp the boat. The tension builds as you pass the first buoy, and you don't relax until you go under the bridge and past Sportsman's Dock, where the river turns south.

That entrance to the harbor is something the fishermen don't get used to, because the degree of danger is never constant. It varies with the tides, with the weather, the surf, and the wind. The channel looks small and there is always some anticipation going in. You look around, sizing up what the conditions might be. If you don't like excitement, you can come to dread it. One fisherman I know gave up fishing, solely because he didn't want to come into that harbor one more time.

There are enough local boats lost coming into Noyo to maintain its mystique, and in other ports the fishermen whose boats are identified with the home port of "Noyo" or "Fort Bragg" are accorded some respect, just by virtue of routinely using that harbor.

To most of the Noyo fishermen, it's an accepted risk and not something we talk about or think about much. It's agreed among most of us that the only time you absolutely can't get into Noyo is when there is a westerly swell, breaking straight in. But there are other conditions when we don't look forward to navigating the channel. Most of us find it remarkable when a boat from Crescent City or San Francisco calls the Coast Guard for an escort in when the weather is relatively calm. But if it is not calm, there are times when local boats wait in the little cove outside the harbor for better entry conditions.

I watched a 60-foot boat sink in the middle of the channel when I was six or seven, along with almost everybody in Fort Bragg. It was just past the jetty, almost all the way in, when a wave broke over the stern and flooded the boat. It had a deck load of fish; there was nowhere for the water to run off, and it began sinking. It took a long time to sink, and as people heard about it they all rushed to Noyo.

I remember it vividly, it was such a somber crowd of people. The only times I had ever seen over a thousand people in one place, it was a parade or a celebration, and everybody was having a good time. The whole population of Noyo and Fort Bragg was there on Noyo beach, or on the road, or on the jetty. About half of them had tears in their eyes, and the other half were pulling on ropes trying to save it.

The Coast Guard was there with the cutter, trying to direct the futile efforts to keep it from sinking. I say trying to because there were a lot of men participating who had their own ideas of what might work, and some of them were trying other desperate measures simultaneously with the official rescue efforts. It didn't matter. You could look in anybody's face that was there on the beach, and you would know the Northern Light was going down.

The Northern Light and the Noyo Star were the aristocrats at Noyo Harbor. They were the two biggest boats at Noyo, and the ones I always looked for. You could always see them if they were in, and I knew where they tied up. Ted Aaker, the owner and skipper of the Northern Light, would always wave back from the big flying bridge if I waved at him. Now he was standing at the end of the spar on top of the Jacob's ladder in water up to his neck, and men were pleading with him to get off the boat. His crewmen were on the Coast Guard boat. I was very scared for him. I wished he would get off.

He had climbed the Jacob's ladder when the water washed over the deck, and then the boat tipped over. He had a wet cigarette in his mouth that he put in it when he started to climb up, but never lit. He was attaching cables, doing whatever anyone told him to do except get off the boat. Most people there knew him, and they were afraid he would never get off the boat. He would never do anything he didn't want to do, and he didn't want to leave his boat.

On the north side, where everybody was gathered pulling on ropes, there was a big tractor and they had attached cables from it to the boat. On the other side of the river by the corner where the jetty wall makes an L-- where the breakers were rolling in--the Union Lumber Company had some equipment they had managed to get down the high bluff at Todd's Point. Every man in town was there, and everybody who had equipment was bringing it. They thought they might be able to save it. Finally, Ted Aaker left the boat when he decided to. There was an audible sigh of relief from all the spectators and participants when he boarded the Coast Guard boat.

All the rescuers were able to do was drag the boat along the river bottom, and they had to stop to avoid causing further damage. Eventually, they raised it with pontoons and it was rebuilt.

That should have been a great day for Ted Aaker. He had a full ice hold and a deck load of salmon. Aaker had been fishing for about 30 years, and had probably risked coming in with a deck load many times before in worse conditions. Many others had, and none of the fishermen were thinking anything except maybe about all the times it might have happened to them. Years later, when I was fishing, I heard somebody say, "Greed sank that boat." I suppressed the impulse to respond and walked away. He wasn't a fisherman.

I suppose knowing all that about the channel takes some of the serenity out of watching the boats come in.

The Dangers

We all know somebody who was lost at sea. You don't get a sense of the numbers unless you're away for ten or fifteen years, and then come back and try to find your old friends. A year or two might pass without a single boat lost. Then a storm will take a toll of two or three. The average is probably two or three men a year lost from this harbor.

I guess it's not so different from cave-ins at a mine, or logging accidents, except that often there's nothing tangible afterward. They're just gone. For a long time you keep watching the sea for them to come home.

On any clear evening there's a gathering of locals and tourists at the Noyo jetty to watch the orange fire of reflected skies as the diminishing cake of sun sinks into the sea on the horizon. It's not a time of socializing. As individuals, couples or groups, each person is silent and alone with the sunset. Except for this daily reenactment of the disappearance of the light, there is no memorial to lost fishermen.

The whole fleet is only a few hundred boats, and the losses are deeply felt. An empty berth in the mooring basin puts a hole in the fleet that we feel and never forget. We all carry the pain of our lost members, but we don't dwell on it. The job has its risks. It's part of the price you pay for living this life.

A memorial would only glorify the dominance of the sea. We wouldn't appreciate it, but I'm sure someday somebody will build one anyway, to make themselves feel better. Then we'll have to look at it, going out and coming in.

We've all heard that crab fishing is the most dangerous job in America, and we don't dispute it. That doesn't keep us from doing it if we want to fish in the winter. We like crab, and sometimes we need the money. Nobody does it because it's exciting and dangerous, any more than a farmer in Bangladesh makes a conscious choice to grow his rice in the path of cyclones. He's exercising his options, just like we are.

We have other options, depending on what we're willing to give up for them. Somebody with a strong need for security will probably find a job on shore. But if you value your independence more highly, there's nothing like fishing. You don't hear fishermen whining, as long as there's some kind of fish to catch.

No fisherman courts danger--not even the young ones eager for adventure like me. The chance of drowning is an occupational hazard, but most fishermen don't end up in the water. The risk is there, and you respect the danger and take precautions, but you don't really think about it much.

Protector of the Fleet--the U.S. Coast Guard

I admired the Coast Guard and probably would have joined up for the adventure and experience at sea, but I had asthma. You don't have to pass a physical to be a fisherman.

There's a Coast Guard station on the south side of the river with a cutter permanently stationed there. Fishermen are independent, perhaps by nature, but certainly by training, and they generally do not like authority. The Coast Guard is the law at Noyo, in the harbor and the sea.

At Noyo, the Coast Guard is looked upon more as protector than authority, to the credit of its captain. Almost everything is at his discretion. He can stop boats from leaving the harbor in uncertain weather. [The Coast Guard chief at Noyo might be called "captain" if he is a lieutenant, "chief" if he is a chief petty officer, or even "boats", or by name, if he is a boatswain mate; it depends on the rank of the person assigned there. The Lieutenant J.G. at this time was called captain.] The captain at Noyo will stop a pleasure boat, but not a fisherman. He respects their judgment when they are risking their lives and their boats.

It takes forbearance for him to watch them go out on choppy seas, because he has to risk his life and his crew if they get in trouble out there. Most of them are sensible, but their caution is tempered by the fact that their livelihood depends on catching fish. But usually if they are out in a storm, it came up while they were already out.

If the Coast Guard captain feels there's too great a risk to his boat and crew, he won't go out. He will not subject his crew to unreasonable risk, but his threshold for what is reasonable is impressively high. If it is possible, a fisherman can count on the Coast Guard to make an effort to rescue him. That commands a high level of respect. At Noyo, you rarely hear anyone criticize the Coast Guard.

A Coast Guard crewman I knew said, "They always told us, 'You have to go out, but you don't have to come back.'" I asked him if he knew that when he joined up. He said, "I guess so. My dad was in the Coast Guard."

He mentioned that he had never figured out whether the captain who was assigned Fort Bragg was being punished or rewarded. It's a challenging assignment, with a large area to patrol and no immediate help when he needs it. The nearest rescue planes are in San Francisco Bay about 105 nautical miles away. Any propeller aircraft rescue would take at least an hour to arrive, and in most situations that would be too late.

I grew up in Fort Bragg, a lumber town a mile north of Noyo and the location of one of the three largest redwood sawmills in the world. The mill and lumber yard takes up all the prime real estate on the ocean bluff, separating the town from the ocean. More than half the residents work there or in the woods, and they know everything there is to know about logging and lumber, and almost nothing about the ocean. It might as well not be there.

Just a mile south, on State Highway 1, where the Noyo River runs into the sea, is the small fishing village where the lives of the other half of Fort Bragg's population are centered, either serving or running the fishing fleet. Most of the fishermen are Italian, Portuguese or Scandinavian, and operate family boats. The majority of them have always fished, and their fathers before them, and uncles and cousins. Some of them don't know where potatoes come from, or anything that doesn't come out of the ocean.

My father worked in the sawmill and I grew up in Fort Bragg, without ever once going out on a boat. My father was more adventuresome than some of the logging contingent, because he took us down to Noyo to watch them unload the boats. Some of the loggers never do that. They look down at Noyo as they drive over the bridge, but they seldom go down the hill.

I've always been fascinated by Noyo. There is an intrigue about it that is intensified by the separateness between the logging and fishing communities.

In any adversity, they are always united. If a boat is sinking near the channel, Union Lumber Company's Caterpillars are mobilized to support it with cables, or pull it off the rocks. If there is a logging accident, the fishermen are at the hospital to donate blood. There is some meeting of the two on the town's volunteer fire department. Except for catastrophe, there's not much contact between the loggers and the fishermen, or their wives. There is mutual respect, but distance.

Logging or sawmill work is not a delicate life, but most of the loggers consider it much safer and saner than fishing. They are not cowards, but most of them wouldn't go out on the ocean for anything. My father has been out a couple of times, against his better judgment, but he isn't in any hurry to try it again.

For as long as I can remember, I watched the boats come in and go out of the harbor, and always wanted to go out on one. I used to go down to Noyo and fish from the docks, and as I got older I started fishing from the jetty. I didn't like to fish that much; I just wanted to go out on one of those boats.

I still get goosebumps thinking about catching my first ling cod off the jetty. It was a giant sea monster, a big, greenish-black creature with bulging eyes and huge fins bristling around its head like an Elizabethan collar. They can be terrifying if you are ten years old and your point of reference is a perch. A crusty old man was sitting about 10 feet away with a gaff hook and a net beside him on a rock. He was watching, but he didn't get up. "Hey sonny, got a gaff?" No. "Too bad. Got a net?" No. "Too bad." He didn't offer to help, and I got mad and landed the fish.

I didn't know it then, but there are many people who consider ling cod the best fish in the ocean. (My dad was one of them.) I carried that fish a few yards down the road and sold him to a man for three dollars. From then on, I'm a fisherman. It's only a matter of time until I will get on a boat.

CHAPTER 2

ON THE DOCKS

Noyo Harbor - 1960-62

While I'm waiting to get on a boat I spend as much time as I can at Noyo. All summer I get up early and ride my bike to Noyo almost every day. I talk to the fishermen working on their boats if they seem receptive. Sometimes I get to help one of them, maybe just by running over to the Noyo Store, the chandlery, to get something he needs. It's like no other store I've ever been inside. It's a big store, crammed with merchandise, but there's not one thing in it that the average person would want. It's full of marine hardware, ropes, netting, and everything related to boats and fishing. The only thing in there that would interest anybody but a fisherman is a small selection of candy bars.

The fishing village is confined to a flat area on both sides of the river, and the larger area on the north side is called "Noyo flat." There are no signs proclaiming it the flat, but that is the native term for it. Most of the fish dealers, businesses and restaurants are on the flat; there are two fish dealers, the Coast Guard station, and a boat builder (Makela brothers) on the opposite side of the river. There is one road along each side; to get to the other side, you have to go back up to Highway 1, across the bridge, out Highway 20, and down the other side--unless you have a rowboat.

By the way, the Chamber of Commerce calls it a "fishing village", but nobody lives there. There are houses along the road leading down to Noyo, but the flat is almost entirely commercial--whatever it takes to serve the fishing fleet.

Along the road and the docks there is a careless collection of buildings and boats, in varying stages of weathered dilapidation or restoration. All the buildings have a muted color unless they have just been painted, because the salt air destroys the paint almost as soon as it is put on. The elements persist until everything is gray, like the fog. There are always some boats on ways being repaired, some being built, and others tied to the docks. The buildings house fish processing plants, boat suppliers, a boat chandlery, a few restaurants, and a Coast Guard station.

Back then, everybody who frequented the flat had at least a nodding acquaintance. They met each other coming and going from Snug Harbor, a coffee shop that would only hold about 15 people at the same time. Fishermen were always making vague plans to meet and fix something on the boat together, and then looking for each other when one of them got around to it, so they came to rely on Snug Harbor. "Tell Charlie I had to run up the hill. I'll be back in about an hour." Finding somebody at Noyo was always like a treasure hunt.

Another place fishermen met was at the diesel shop, or the fuel and ice dock where they also had a small chandlery, or the Noyo Store, a bigger chandlery. I started getting cokes and coffee at Snug Harbor and loitering around the suppliers' docks when I decided I wanted to learn fishing. I was too young to hang out in bars--and you don't find many fishermen in bars anyway, unless they're blown in at a harbor away from home and have nothing to do.

The sixties are prosperous times for salmon and albacore fishermen, and Noyo is an exciting place to be. There is activity everywhere on the flat, beginning about four in the morning. There's an infectious excitement as the boats go out in the early morning and come back in loaded heavily with fish. Summer is the height of the salmon season, and some of the fishermen make their income for the whole year from salmon.

There's always a din. You hear ice machines running, ice crashing into containers, diesels starting, people swearing in several languages, and always the high-pitched cries of the sea gulls, like a cat's meow but louder and more demanding. The air smells like salt and something else...crab cocktail, clam chowder, fresh coffee, and maybe a light hint of diesel--not a bad smell.

I stand around the processing plants, watching men and women in boots and yellow oilcloth aprons, cleaning and filleting fish at long tables. I watch them push around huge bins of ice and piles of fish, and hose the concrete floors, patterned with gutters and drains. Water is always running on the tables and on the floor, and I always get wet, but I keep out of the way. Sometimes one of the workers gives me a bag of salmon cheeks to take home. Those are a delicacy, deep fried or grilled--bite-sized salmon rounds with no bones. They're free because they don't process them; it's too expensive and time-consuming, so they're fringe benefits for the dock workers.

When there are big loads of bottom fish, the fish houses are busy and call in extra help. Some of the women on call are wives of fishermen, or their friends or neighbors. My aunt works there sometimes; one of her friends is married to a fisherman. She likes making some extra money, and the socializing during breaks. She also likes the competition, because she and her friends are fast and enjoy being better at it than some of the others. They get paid by how much they do, not by the hour.

None of them like working in crab or shrimp. Fresh fish has no odor, but she can never get the smell of crab or shrimp off her hands or out of her hair. They all wear their hair wrapped in bandanas, but that doesn't seem to matter. My uncle complains about that, because he doesn't like her working there. He's a lumber man. He builds boats as a hobby, but doesn't like going out on them. Once he launches it and tests it out, he's through; he sells it and builds another one.

On a busy day at the Grader Fish Company, I see a big, burly man handling salmon at one of the fillet tables. Under the table at his feet is a small boy about three years old, immobile, with the man's foot firmly on his shirt. The child is pouty, but not crying, sitting there on the wet concrete. A woman, who looks shocked, asks the man if it's his child. It isn't; someone left the little boy to play on the docks and went to get a cup of coffee, or maybe a drink. It's almost a 20-foot drop to the water, and there are no bottom barriers on the railings. "I've pulled him out of the water once today, and I'm not going to do it again." A woman finally comes and rescues the little boy. I'm out of range, so I don't hear the brief exchange, but I'm sure it's spicy.

I gradually get acquainted with some of the fishermen and dock workers. Before long, I know every foot of the docks behind the processing plants. I stand back watching the dock workers as they unload the boats. They lower large wooden boxes on winches down 15 or 20 feet to the boats below. The crewmen fill the boxes from the ice hold, and the boxes are hoisted back up. The fish are put on scales, tallied, and then put into big carts of ice and wheeled inside.

If it is a small or moderate catch, the salmon are already sorted by size and cleaned. If the hold is full, the fishermen don't bother to sort them. When there is that much action, there isn't time to put them away that neatly. Besides, the highliners--the fishermen who catch more fish, consistently, than anyone else--like dazzling people with their catch.

They are always cleaned, though. No fisherman would be so disrespectful of his home harbor to clean fish in the port. If things were so hectic that they didn't have a chance to clean the fish, they would anchor outside in the bay until they were cleaned. Only a sport fisherman would clean fish in the harbor.

The boats usually come in in the late afternoon. There are always people from town to watch them unload. The skipper enjoys the attention, unloading several thousand dollars worth of fish. It always awes the mill workers, who never get that much money at one time. They see the salmon as so many silver dollars, not thinking of the weeks and months the fisherman never sees a paycheck. Most of the locals think all fishermen with big boats are rich, because the boats cost so much. In fact, many of the boats are mortgaged to the fish house.

Nearly every fisherman is living for the day he can buy his own boat, unless he has one. Then he is living for the day he can pay off his mortgage and buy a better boat. Except for the few who have made it big and bought a Makela brothers boat. They are just hoping that nothing bad happens to it. The Makela brothers, Fred and Nick, build the ultimate wooden boats at Noyo. I like to watch those unload, just to get a look at them.

Hardly anyone becomes a fisherman deliberately. Most of them are born to it because there is a family boat. I knew it would be as difficult for me to get on a boat as it is for some of my friends, who don't especially like the life, to avoid it.

With no experience there was no chance of getting hired as a crewman. There is room for only two or three people on those boats, and they had better know how to fish. I wouldn't make anybody much money on what I know. So I do some other things around the river for a while and get to know something about the fringes. There is more to know than you would think.

When I'm 14, Tony Marino, who runs a fish house on the other side of the river, gives me my first summer job. He's probably tired of seeing me hanging around doing nothing. This is my big break, because everybody's kid wants a job at Noyo and there are not enough to go around. Not only am I not related to a fisherman; I'm not even Italian. So I really appreciate it. They stack albacore on the floor, like cord wood; so at first my main duties are stacking albacore, shoveling ice, and scrubbing the floors thoroughly every night with rock salt, and hosing them down with a fire hose. We couldn't use any chemicals on the floor, because the fish were in contact with it, but rock salt worked surprisingly well. It had to be clean enough to eat from; if it wasn't clean enough for Tony, I got to do it again; but I made sure that never happened more than once.

When I'm finally old enough to be a dock worker and handle a knife, Tony promotes me to a slimer. The job is as bad as it sounds. There are four of us. We start at five in the morning, and our job is to trim the fins off salmon and clean them up and pack them in barrels of brine after Tony splits them for lox. The first day I cut my left thumb across the knuckle about twenty times.

Tony tells us everything we need to know, once; and he teaches us how to sharpen our knives. He tells us once that if we don't keep them sharp, we will cut ourselves. When we do, he says, "Your knife is dull." After a couple of hours, we learn to stop about every five minutes and touch it up with a steel, to keep it from getting dull.

Tony obviously believes experience is the best teacher, so the one who cuts himself the most any one day has the job of packing the fish in rock salt. He's like a shop teacher, pouring alcohol over a cut you wouldn't have got if you were holding your chisel right. It's extremely painful, and it takes about two hours to finish packing the fish. We have a normal rotation for it whenever nobody cuts themselves.

Because of the salt, it will leave a scar deeper and wider than the cut would have been, and it hurts like hell until the packing is done. We have to do the trimming with a constant stream of cold water running over the salmon, so there is no way to stop the bleeding from a cut--or hide it from Tony. That soon becomes more important than losing a pint of blood.

When you trim the thin piece of skin across the belly of a split salmon side, your thumb is perilously close to the knife blade, depending on how much nail you have on your thumb and index finger--and you'd better have some. Speed is of the essence in sliming. We're paid by the hour, but our boss is standing right over us, drinking coffee and smoking a cigarette, waiting for the four of us to catch up with him. He can clean a side of salmon in a little under three seconds. You do all the handling of the fish with your left hand, because you never put your knife down. You can get pretty hacked up while you're getting the hang of it.

Another disadvantage to the job is that you can get blood poisoning handling fish when you have open cuts. We have some black, oily salve that is a favorite of fishermen. It has iodine in it and burns like fire, but it keeps the cut open and draws the poison out. You don't use it if you are concerned about scars. The salt helps too. We don't have to worry about infection, only the size of the scars.

At first, I'm not sure I'm going to make it as a slimer. When you get stuck by a fin or a spine, about ten minutes later a sensation comes over you like you're shot by a poison dart. There is immediate nausea and dizziness, and you think you're going to die. In half an hour or so, the sickness is gone. It bothers you a little less when you know it's going to go away.

In record time, I learn how to trim fins, cut away skin, and scrape the sides and backs to get the blood out of the veins without further deforming my hands. By then I have skin on them like burned and mangled leather, but they are starting to heal. For several months, anyone who looks at them quickly looks away with an expression of horror. I'm almost proud of the scars around my friends, because they make me seem tough; but I'm ashamed of them around Tony.

Splitting a salmon is like filleting except it's a full-size, full-length half of a salmon, skinned and boned. (And why would a Portuguese or Italian fisherman use a fancy French word? They don't.) This may be more than you wanted to know, but if you did want to learn how to properly split a salmon for lox, there's only a handful of people in the world you could ask. Skip this part if you want, but if you read it, and later you see a fisherman with a big grin holding up a salmon and saying, "It's a splitter", you'll know what he's talking about.

I don't fully appreciate Tony's talents as a salmon splitter until I find out there are only five or six people on the west coast who can do it. They don't train salmon splitters. Not because they don't want them to learn, but because it takes years to learn to do it right. They estimate that it costs ten thousand dollars in wasted fish to train a splitter, with salmon under a dollar a pound.

There is one other expert splitter at Noyo, at Paladini's, a fish house on the other side of the river. Every few years, he and Tony have a contest to see how many salmon they can split in an hour. It got started one year when somebody from Paladini's was bragging about how fast Joe could split salmon. Tony splits about sixty and wins every time, by three or four fish. Joe isn't bad-- but the bones on Tony's salmon are perfectly white. There isn't much pink on Joe's, but you can tell they are salmon. That's the difference.

Tony is one of those people you look up to the first time you meet him, and then one day you are shocked to realize he is under five feet tall. You might not notice it for months. After you do, you are just more impressed with him.

Tony keeps four of us busy trimming, and he often has to stop and wait for us to catch up. It's fascinating to watch him. It's fascinating for me to watch anybody do anything with that much finesse.

Only the big king salmon are split, although they would split silvers if the kings were scarce. All the splitters are over ten pounds. Tony does the splitting first thing in the morning. Salmon are delicate fish, and they are handled and cleaned carefully so they won't get bruised. When the fishermen clean them, they stop short of the gills with the cut so that they won't spread open in the ice hold and get bruised or torn. The meticulous fishermen are careful to get all the blood out so it won't turn black. The heads are never cut off until they reach the fish house. They are important for measuring and handling. Tony selects the best fish to split for lox.

The knife he uses for splitting has a tip shaped like a machete, and it's sharp all the way along the rounded tip. You could shave with it easily, if you were allowed to pick it up; we can't even touch it.

There is a small hook embedded in the table, like a bent nail, where Tony hooks the fish's head during the splitting procedure. When he splits a salmon, the fish is flat in front of him, with its head on his right. He starts the split at the fin behind the dorsal fin, between the dorsal fin and the tail. He inserts the knife through that fin, on the back of the fish, clear through the fish, over the backbone and as close to the backbone as he can get it. He holds both hands on the knife handle and puts pressure downward on the knife blade against the bone and in one, quick snap he splits it from that point back.

Then he goes to the head, right at the top of the gill curve, and cuts straight down to the backbone, then turns the knife and gets it started toward the tail of the fish. Then, with both hands on the knife, he presses downward and one swipe toward the tail finishes the process. That takes off one side of the fish.

The fish's right side is called a "side"; the other is called a "back". Tony takes the back and inserts the knife in the same place, by that corresponding fin, and makes one sweeping motion pressing up on the knife blade. The knife comes completely out at the tail. Then he turns the fish over and cuts down, straight back again and toward the backbone. That leaves him with nothing but a backbone and head, with nothing on the backbone, in much less time than I can describe it.

Then we have to trim off the fins and loose skin, and clean out any blood from the backs and sides Tony has split. We have to get them spiffed up and spotless, and pack them in barrels of brine. An 800-pound barrel, packed solid, is worth $1,100 a barrel wholesale. It is prime.

When Tony is through splitting salmon, he runs the river from a little office upstairs. He is the contact for all the available trucks and dispatches them where they are needed, to the other fish houses. If anybody needs a truck, they have to ask Tony. A truck can be very critical when you have a bonanza like a deck load of fish and a full ice hold. Fish are not worth much if they lay around too long.

Tony leaves us with the job of getting the lox ready to ship. The barrels are like wine barrels, about four feet high and three feet wide in the center. They have six rings, and two have to be taken off to get the lid on. If there is a small leak, we fix it by coopering the rings with a hammer and a set. A bad leak has to be caulked like a boat seam.

We pack the fish in a circular motion, sides and backs alternated against the side of the barrel, two in the middle, then two in the opposite direction, keeping them level. There are three of us doing this, while the other takes them out of the fish buggy and puts them carefully in the salt box. It's like a sandbox on legs. The buggies are like garden carts, scaled up. The wheels are three feet in diameter, and the carts are perfectly balanced. Each one holds more than 800 pounds of fish, and one person can dump it.

The salter has to make a forearm sweep to keep the salt smooth so the side gets uniformly salted. Then he has to sweep the salt over the salmon side. That's when his cuts smart. Then, when the barrels are packed, we fill them with brine and leave them overnight. The next day we check each one for leaks, patch it if necessary, and then dump the first day's brine and refill it with brine. We roll them over on their sides for a few days until we are absolutely sure there are no leaks. It's always a couple of weeks before any are shipped out to the east coast.

Every day we have to put two sacks of salt into the brine tanks. There is no pump, the tanks are gravity fed, so they are mounted on high racks on the outside wall of the building, reached by a narrow stairway with no railing. The salt is packed like cement; rock salt about the size of pea gravel in 100-pound sacks. It's a killer to carry those sacks up the narrow steps and pour them slowly into the tanks. Of course, we do it one at a time. I tried to lift two of them once, and I could get both on my shoulders but I didn't try to walk with them. You had to keep your muscles tight, or you could really hurt yourself. It was a challenge handling one.

There was no place to put it down once you got up there, so you stood on the top step with the brine barrel chest level at the end of the platform. Then you had to open the sack with it still on your shoulder; there was a laced string that pulled easily. Then you had to pour it in slowly to avoid raising sediment or forcing weaker brine to the surface.

Jim, the biggest and strongest slimer, was 6'6" tall and could easily handle the salt sacks, but he always was busy when it had to be done. He was the first to grab easier jobs that took a lot of time. It would have taken him about a minute to put salt in the brine barrel. When he did do it, rarely, he would stagger over the weight of one sack.

One day Tony gets tired of watching this game. He goes over to the pallet, puts his head between two salt sacks, puts one arm around each, bends his knees and picks them up, and straightens up quickly to get them on his shoulders. Then he walks up the stairs to the top with both of them, leans against the wall, opens the one on the left and dumps it in the barrel slowly. Then he opens the other one and dumps it in slowly. Then Tony comes down the stairs and walks off shaking his head in disgust. He was teaching Jim a lesson. This brand of subtlety is a cultural trait among the old Italians around Noyo. After that, Tony started picking on Jim more and working him pretty hard, but he had it coming. He responded by appearing to work hard whenever Tony was around.

Finally, they have a confrontation. Everybody is exhausted from unloading boats. The weather came up, so the whole Sausalito mosquito fleet came in. It's a fleet of Monterey Clippers, classic west coast double enders that are rounded at bow and stern, that fish together out of Sausalito. We were unloading a boat every five minutes in a steady stream all day.

It was work getting them lined up to the hoist. Some of them coast into the dock, throw you a line, and kill the engine at the same time. The more considerate ones line up to the dock and then shut off the engine.

When we're finally through, Tony is really down on Jim for not doing his share. It started out as good-natured kidding, Tony telling Jim how lazy he was, and Jim talking back and calling Tony a slave driver.

Jim would be straining and groaning over stacking a fish box, as if it were really heavy. The order was stamped on the end, so if you looked at that you could see it only had three fish in it. He wasn't fooling us, and he certainly wasn't fooling Tony. The rest of us bitched at him a little, but not too much because Jim was big. He was throwing ice at us, and he hit Tony in the face with a handful of bloody ice.

"You s.o.b.–I ought to throw you in the river."

"You ain't big enough, you little wop."

Jim shouldn't have said that, because it was about 20 feet to the water from that dock. If you're unprepared, it's a long way to do a belly flop. Tony picked him up by the seat of the pants and the back of his shirt, and actually lifted him off the dock and clear of the railing. Jim hit the water hard. But he climbed up the ladder and worked until nine that night in wet clothes.

Jim has a lot of respect for Tony; everybody does. He doesn't get down on anybody too much, but he lets you know if you're not cutting it. If a drag boat comes in unexpectedly late at night, Tony will call me or one of the other guys. Jim doesn't get the extra work. When he proves himself, he will--if that ever happens.

Unloading boats is my favorite part of this job. That's how I get to know the fishermen. Whenever we hear a boat chugging up to the dock, or see one coming, we drop everything--sometimes literally. Once day I have a cigarette in one hand and a cup of coffee in the other, and a skipper throws me his rope to tie up. I drop both, and catch it. It's "Killer Willie", one of the top highliners fishing out of Noyo. He isn't exactly arrogant; he just considers his job done when he brings in the fish. When he comes up to the dock, he doesn't even try to position the boat conveniently. He just shuts off the engine and lets us pull the boat in and line it up.

Tony always comes down from his office when Willie or any of the other highliners come in, and gives them his personal attention. He weighs their fish himself. There is some competition among the dealers to keep highliners, and they are catered to. They expect it. Tony is the one with the authority to sort the fish a bit more favorably for the fisherman when a fish is on the borderline between small, medium, or large. There are three different rates per pound, large being the most expensive.

Tony has a helper who can man the hoist if he can't be there, but Tony takes charge of unloading the boats whenever he can, no matter who brings in the fish. The dealer makes his profit right there at the scale, along with the fisherman. In any business, somebody will find a way to cheat, and fishing is no exception. If a fisherman leaves ice in the bellies of the salmon, you'll be paying them $1 a pound for ice. If they try to sneak in an illegal size fish because it was dead or wouldn't survive if released, the dealer can get in as much trouble as they can. If a king salmon is 25-3/4 inches when 26 is legal, it's okay to squeeze the tail while holding the fish against the rule. But it is not legal to break its spine or pull the vertebrae apart to actually stretch it. That's almost impossible to tell; Tony could tell. Steelhead are illegal commercially, and they're hard to tell from silvers; but not for Tony.

You could tell if Tony didn't like somebody on the boat who was sending up the fish. Normally he would let the bucket drain out before he sent it back down. If he didn't, fish slime and icy salt water would run down their necks as they caught the bucket to refill it in the ice hold. There would be swearing and apologies. That happened rarely, but Tony was never careless. You knew he had a good reason.

For his regular fishermen, a good splitter that was 9-3/4 pounds would go with the large (10 lb. and above) instead of the medium. For a splitter, weight doesn't matter to a dealer, but a 30 to 40 cent per pound difference matters a lot to the fisherman. Mediums were 7 to 9 pounds; smalls were 6 or under. For a transient fleet, the dealers sorted strictly by the rules, to the letter.

There are about five fish dealers on the river besides Tony. Two of them have plants in San Francisco and Sausalito as well as Noyo. The others are local, about the same scale as Tony's operation, except for one smaller independent. The fishermen can sell to anybody, but they stay with one dealer as long as they are treated well. The smallest dealer pays higher prices. The others all belong to the Salmon Trollers Association and agree on the prices at the start of the season.

There is some advantage to the fishermen to stay with one dealer. If they are regulars, the dealer will see that they always get the best bait, and enough bait, even when it is in short supply. Some years there are not enough herring, and then it's difficult to get good bait unless you have clout with somebody. If you have to use old, frozen bait you just don't do as well. Tony takes good care of "his" boats. If he knows that one of them is not going to be in until 9 o'clock at night, he will keep the fish house open until it arrives.

I learn quite a lot about the business working for Tony, just from exposure. When there is a squabble between Tony and a fisherman, or one of the other dealers, it takes place at an elevated pitch and volume right on the docks in front of you or up in Tony's open office. It isn't like some businesses where differences are discussed privately or quietly. Normally, you hear everything that is going on.

I'm grateful to Tony for the job, because it gets me closer to the chance to go fishing, but the longer I work there and look down on those boats, the more I want to be on one of them. I still don't know how to fish, but I'm established as a hard worker because I work for Tony. I let the fishermen know I'm available, and Tony knows I'll take the first opportunity that comes along to join a crew.

One of Tony's regulars is a fisherman named Rudy Salinnen. Rudy has a small boat, and he often fishes alone. He's not a highliner, but Tony and the other fishermen have a lot of respect for him and treat him like one. Once Tony told me that Rudy learned the coastline in a 12-foot skiff as a boy. One of the highliners said Rudy would beat them all if he ever decided to take fishing seriously. Rudy's goals in life are not highly material, and he always has time to talk to me about fishing. One day he says, "Hey, Pat. You still want to go fishing?" I did.

I break the happy news to Tony, and he calls some other poor slob on the waiting list aspiring to the hapless training period of a slimer. I feel a twinge of sympathy for his hands. I finish out the day, and then begin to prepare myself to be a fisherman.

First I have to get a commercial license. You don't touch a fishing boat unless you're a dock worker or have a commercial license. You can even get in trouble if you're standing on the dock and touch a rope to tie up a boat. The dealers enforce it, because the fishermen are so adamant about it. Every crewman who has to pay for a commercial license wants to be sure that anyone else who steps aboard a boat does too. For all I know, I might get sick the first day and decide it isn't for me. Nevertheless, I have to get a license to even try it. Incidentally, it doesn't even cross my mind that I might get sick. It might have occurred to Rudy but, if so, he doesn't mention it.

Rudy gives me some fundamental advice before I buy my boots. He says to be sure to get them loose--at least two sizes too big--so I can kick them off if I need to. I had noticed fishermen's boots were always too big, and I thought they were sloppy. I didn't tell Rudy, but one of my looked-forward-to distinctions as a fisherman was to have boots that fit. Now I understand. I buy mine two sizes too big, like any sensible fisherman.

CHAPTER 3

MASTER FISHERMAN

If you're looking at it in the harbor, a 35-foot fishing boat seems fairly large, but when you take it out on the turbulent Pacific--the world's largest pond--you see it for the nutshell craft that it is. The Pacific Ocean covers an area of about 67 million square miles, give or take. We cover maybe 400 square feet of it.

Spring 1965

State of the art in marine electronics:
Scanners haven't been invented yet--CB radios get one channel at a time; radar is available but too expensive for most small boats;
Long Range Navigation (Loran) is primitive and there are few Loran stations. Satellite navigation, which enables Global Positioning Satellite systems (GPS) for boats, is still science fiction.

Rudy knows I've never been out on a boat. I think he decided to give me a chance based on my enthusiasm, and partly for the company. It's a calculated risk for him whether he will make more money with help, or a little less. If the fish are plentiful, he stands to make considerably more with my help than he could alone; two people can bring in a lot more fish. But if the fish aren't there, he'll probably make a little less. The going rate for a crewman is fifteen percent of the catch. He doesn't absolutely need help, but it's easier if there is somebody else to steer the boat or handle the gear. Since I don't know how to do either, we agree that I will start for ten percent.

Rudy says to meet him at seven in the morning at his boat. I am the most enthusiastic crewman ever; I'm there at six. That gives me a lot of time to look over the boat with my new perspective. This is the vehicle for my first trip out on the ocean, and I look at it with keen interest in every detail.

I already know from conversations with Rudy that he gives up very little of his freedom to acquire anything, and this is reflected in his boat. It's the most seaworthy boat you can buy for practically nothing. The "Driftwood" is a 35-foot double-ender, a converted World War II Captain's gig. During the war they were launched from ships to carry the captain or passengers from one ship to another, or to shore. Rudy has modified it, primarily by adding a small cabin and salmon rigging. Otherwise, it looks much like it always has, though it has lost its military spiffiness.

I liked the feel of the boat as soon as I stepped on board. It was small, but solidly built. I had been in rowboats and canoes and small sailboats, but never on a boat so solid and stable. There is something reassuring and natural about the feel of a well built wooden boat. It was the simplest of classic boats, cedar on oak ribs with copper fittings.

It didn't take me long to look around. There wasn't much area to cover. The cabin had a sliding door facing the stern. I stepped inside, and two steps in any direction would have put me across the cabin. A big man could have touched both sides of it. Fortunately, Rudy and I were both small. The cabin was about the size of a small bathroom, but seemed bigger because of the windows on three sides. There was nothing much in the wheel house. The wheel was on the left side, and the radio, compass and fathometer were next to it. To the right there were steps leading down to the foc's'le. Down the steps there was a small wood stove and bunks built in a v-shape right into the bow of the boat. The engine was there, too. That was it below deck.

Rudy drives up in his van and, instead of getting out, he motions for me to get in. He drives over to Snug Harbor and gets us coffee, and then drives up the road away from Noyo, across the bridge, and out onto the point. He says he always likes to see how it looks before he goes out.

I don't know what he's looking for, but he's probably checking to see if there are any white caps, making sure it isn't going to blow. It's a little windy on the point. Apparently he is satisfied with what he sees, because he drives back down the hill to Noyo and parks the van to go fishing. I help him carry some bait and sinkers from the van, and he comes on board with a small box of groceries containing crackers, bread, salami and cheese, and two gallon jugs of red wine.

Rudy puts the groceries in the cabin and shows me how to start the engine. It doesn't start right away, so he kicks it in a vulnerable place where he knows the malfunction is centered, and it starts right up. He tells me what the problem is, and says he has the new part on board. He assures me he could fix it if he ever had to. This was my first glimpse of one of Rudy's strongest character traits that made fishing with him interesting: he rarely fixed anything until he had to. Then he always did.

He had an extra radio that was broken, but he thought he could fix it if he had to. He never tried. He probably couldn't fix it unless he just had to. Then maybe he could. Probably. I could understand that.

Finally, we're going down the river past the docks. It's exciting for me when we get to the jetty where I stood so often watching boats go out. It's hard to believe I am actually on one of them.

Despite the fact that the Driftwood is one of the smallest boats in the river, I feel safe going out with Rudy. I'd be going, whether I felt safe or not. I've been waiting for this a long time.

I'm not sure that I want to be a fisherman. I have no concept at all of what it's like. I just want to try it. I know I don't want to do any of the other things I can think of that I might do instead. I don't want to sit at a desk, or work in the mill or in the woods, or sell insurance or cars. I don't want to sit in college and learn what other people think about the world. I want to do things, and learn from scratch, and make my own observations. At least I want to do some of that first, before anybody else tells me what to think.

Part of the attraction is the sense of adventure. Like most 17-year-olds, I feel invincible. But mostly, I start fishing because I've always wanted to go out to sea on a boat and find out what it's like.

The ocean looks smooth, so I am surprised at how much motion there is once we get outside the channel. At first, when the boat comes down off a swell it hits the water with a hard slap. Rudy slows down, and then it only rocks with them, but there is still more motion than I expected. I have trouble with my footing. I wonder how you can do anything with the floor under you so unpredictable, but eventually I get used to it.

I don't fully appreciate the value of an apprenticeship with Rudy Salinnen, because I have no basis for comparison. I don't know what is on the other boats, or what other fishermen know, or how they fish. I will learn that every skipper I ever fish with in the future will just increase my respect for Rudy, even though I will respect some of them as much in other ways. For basic navigation and for finding and catching fish--without any aids--none of them will ever come close to Rudy.

Contrary to what you might have heard, fishing is the oldest profession. Rudy had centuries of seamanship coursing through his veins, and that was primarily what he relied on out in the ocean. His heritage could be traced to the sea as far back as it could be traced. His grandfather was captain of one of the "dog hole schooners" that delivered lumber, supplies and passengers to the small ports up and down the coast. His father was captain of a two-masted schooner he sailed here from Norway. Rudy started fishing on his uncle's boat when he was nine or ten, after exploring the coast in a skiff when he was too young to fish. It was like fishing with Neptune, himself. The ocean was his element.

Most of the boats at Noyo have sophisticated electronic equipment on them that cost more than the boats. Some of the bigger, more expensive boats have all their equipment duplicated so there is no down time in case of a failure. Some highliners have as many as four radios to monitor more fishing conversations. They have radios, fathometers, hydraulic anchor winches, Loran (long range navigation) for direction-finding, radar for the fog, and a lot of them have automatic pilot. Some of the boats even have equipment for fish-finding. There is an echo sounder for depth, and sonar is just developing for horizontal searching.

Loran at this time is not yet a very sophisticated system. The most common are ex-military units. Accuracy is fairly good for latitude here, but the signals are too weak to provide reliable reading for longitude because the nearest Loran station is in Hawaii. This causes boats that rely on it too heavily to steam full-speed into the rocks in thick fog, believing they are still miles from shore. You hear of a lot more boats running on the rocks since they got Loran than before it was available. But it's valuable if you don't get too dependent on it to judge how far you are from shore. Most fishermen won't even consider going out if their Loran isn't working. Rudy doesn't have one.

Some of the boats even have automatic distress signals. Nearly all of them have life rafts with CO_2 cartridges that trigger when a sensor fills with water, to blow them clear of the rigging. Rudy has one of those, because he says it's foolish not to have one as long as they are available.

To Rudy, those other things are about as important as an electric can opener. They are nice to have, but definitely frills. He has a compass, a radio and a fathometer. He pulls his anchor by hand. The fathometer saves him the trouble of putting down a line periodically to check the depth. The radio is for emergencies, but it also helps to know what is going on out there. Sometimes you can find out where somebody is catching fish. But what he has, he has for its convenience; he doesn't need any of it.

If I had fished with anybody else first, I would have been dependent on some of those devices and very insecure without them. Fortunately, I haven't, so I don't know how unusual it is to navigate by your senses, as Rudy does.

As we are going out to the fishing grounds, Rudy explains some things about the configuration of the bottom in certain places, and how you can figure out where you are by checking the depth. Rudy knows the depth of the water all along the coast, and he usually knows exactly where we are by the patterns to the depth. The bottom varies north and south of Noyo from 18 to 25 fathoms when you're out past the buoys. Off Point Cabrillo it's 45 fathoms. He stresses that it is always more important to know you are out far enough, beyond the rocks, than it is to know precisely where you are out here. "That only becomes important when you're ready to come in."

I'm surprised how hard it is to identify anything on land, as familiar as I am with the shore. The only thing I recognize are unmistakable landmarks, like the smoke stacks at the mill. It's useless to look at the rocks and try to tell anything.

I think I have his undivided attention, but I learn later that as he is talking he's making mental notes of the boat speed, the wind speed, currents, and depth. He is always noticing a wide range of variables, and keeping close track of where we are, even as he is telling me it's unimportant to know. He always has a rough idea of where we are, within about five miles.

I never see Rudy concerned about our exact location. Dead reckoning is good enough for him. He is unconcerned even in the fog. He always says the bigger danger is going into the rocks. If you're out far enough, there is no danger of that; so why worry about where you are. He doesn't waste any fishing time trying to figure it out precisely. I get comfortable with that, but I learn soon enough that it isn't common among fishermen.

Other boats are always trying to check their precise location with us on the radio. I'm sure it frustrates them when Rudy says, "Yeah, that must be about right." Most of them, especially the younger ones, don't deal in "abouts". Verifying your Loran reading with Rudy is like setting your watch by a sundial. Some of the older ones have more confidence in Rudy's best guess than they do in another skipper's ability to read his Loran. If their equipment doesn't seem right they will check their bearings with Rudy if they can see us, regardless of who else with elaborate equipment is around.

The thing Rudy stresses most that first day out is safety in handling the salmon gear. He had insisted that a sheath knife was a necessity, so I had bought one. He explains what can happen if a hook gets caught in your hand when it's still attached to a leader on the main line. There is a 50-pound weight on the end of that line, on 100-pound test leader. The lines are controlled by gurdies (gears and reels). The lines from the gurdies go to pulleys mounted on a bent pipe called a davit. If the gurdy is knocked out of gear, the line goes down fast and can take you with it. You want to have something to cut the leader, on the boat or on the way down. When I see how fast it goes down, I'm glad I have the knife.

Salmon gear is designed for trolling deep in relatively shallow water, compared with albacore. Salmon are caught within the continental shelf, sometimes very close to shore, and albacore are usually farther out in deep waters, as much as 200 miles or more offshore. But salmon stay at a greater depth than albacore, which feed at the surface. Salmon trolling speed is about one to one and a half knots, because the herring they feed on are relatively slow moving fish.

The gear is trolled from outriggers to keep the lines apart, but nobody calls them outriggers. We call them poles, but they're not fishing poles; they are the 40 to 60-foot poles you see standing straight up on each side of the mast when boats are in port. When we extend them out each side of the boat for trolling, the boats look like giant grasshoppers, from a distance. From each pole, tag lines a few feet apart suspend the clothespin line snaps that hold the lines and leaders.

Salmon gear is mechanized, and Rudy's is arranged so that one person can control the boat, run the gurdy, and handle the catch. When the tops of the poles jerk, you know a fish is hooked. Then you activate the hydraulic gurdy for that line and haul in the line. When the insulator holding the line reaches the edge of the boat, you unsnap the empty leaders as they are brought alongside. When you reach the leader with the fish, you haul it in by hand until you can gaff it and bring it on board.

The other thing Rudy cautions me about is holding onto the stainless steel wire that holds the leaders, because if it has breaks in it you can cut yourself. But, worse, if you are having trouble unhooking the leader and hold on too long, the pulley can take your finger off when it gets up there.

Rudy shows me how to unhook a leader from the main line when a salmon is on, and to hook it on a 2-foot long rubber band on the back of the boat, that he calls a "rubber snubber." (That may be a unique Noyo term--I don't know because I've never fished anywhere else.) The reason for that is if you hooked it to something solid while you were playing a salmon, the fish might stop short and snap off, sending the hook right back at you. Rudy says that is the most dangerous thing out here. If a fish gets off when it is hooked to the rubber snubber, you have to duck--but you're expecting it.

When Rudy puts so much emphasis on what can be dangerous, I'm almost too cautious with the gear at first. Later, when it is familiar and I handle it far more casually, I'm always aware of those dangers. I never get careless about those things.

It takes me years to fully appreciate just how basic and significant his instruction is. After we get out and start fishing, he teaches me things about handling the bait and gear that I never would have learned in years of fishing. Whenever I am fishing with somebody else, I always feel one up on them just for having fished with Rudy.

Silver salmon are not picky, and most of the fishermen start the season the first couple of weeks with hardware ("junk") instead of bait fish. Later when the kings start running, you're not going to catch them with junk, or even dragging a dead fish through the water. The eyes have to be the right color, and you have to put it on the hook so it has the look and action of a live fish. At certain times of the year salmon bite real short. You get scratched bait, and no fish. When that happens, Rudy shows me how to cut the scratched tails off and pull the spine and tail out so nothing sticks out past the bend of the hook. Then we catch fish. Rudy teaches me tricks with the bait that I never saw done on any other boat later on.

We catch some big salmon that first day out, and I learn how to gaff and land them, although I lose one medium-sized one. The first few trips are just day trips, because the salmon are running close in. By the third trip, I know how to fish and how to steer, and Rudy is paying me fifteen percent.

I enjoy the radio chatter out here. Rudy explains the codes fishermen devise when they are trying to tell a friend where they are catching a lot of fish, without telling everybody else. When they all figure one out, everybody runs to one spot and you expend more effort dodging lines from other boats than fishing.

One common method for tipping off friends is to use a landmark boat. The Smith brothers boat is painted bright orange and black, like the cough drop box, so it is the obvious landmark if it is in view. Everyone code-names it (not too subtly) "the great pumpkin". It has a big flying bridge that extends two stories above the deck and high out of the water. Anybody within range can see it. Someone will come on the radio and say, "We're catching a few fish about a quarter-mile southeast of the great pumpkin." If you are a few miles away and can't see that boat, it doesn't tell you anything. But it's valuable information for the fishermen on the orange boat; they are always in the fish.

You get to know everybody out there with you, but not the name of the boat, or what boat the voice is coming from. You never ask another fisherman what gear or bait he's using. One of them might mention what color jigs, if nobody else is around. You hear a lot of codes for giving their position to a friend. Someone will come on the radio and say, "5, 4, 3, 2, 1--out."

Nobody ever says they are catching a lot of fish. Somebody might say they are catching three or four an hour. A friend might answer that they are catching five or six, it might be a little better spot. When they say that, they are probably pulling them in as fast as they can.

Nobody ever sounds excited, and the tips are understated. You don't believe them about anything but weather or position. You don't know what they've got until they come in and unload. Somebody always sees them unload, and the word gets around.

Rudy rarely talks on the radio. He will answer if he is addressed, but he almost never initiates a conversation on the radio. He just listens. He always helps nearby boats if he is doing well, but with hand signals instead of the radio because he wants to share, but not bring the whole fleet down around him. If you put one of these guys onto the fish when he's not catching them, that little favor will be repaid--but it's hard to do. I notice that whenever we help somebody by directing them to the fish, they always remember and find a way to repay us when they are doing well.

There's one Portuguese fisherman who has a real struggle keeping his language groomed for the radio. His normal expression is peppered with minor cussing by habit. He has to suppress half his vocabulary to talk on the radio, and he often forgets. Sometimes a "sonofabitch" slips in, and he gets a ticket from the FCC in Washington with a $50 fine.

The radio equipment on the boats varies all over the place. The extremes might have three VHF sets, two CBs, and a couple of AM short wave radios: more money in the wheel house than they have in the rest of the boat, including the gear. A few have AM radios more powerful than 50 to 100-watt radio stations. These powerful AM transmitters have signals that can "skip" halfway around the world and interfere with air traffic controllers in Holland. The FCC is trying to bring some order to the airwaves and abolish these ultra-powerful AM transmitters.

Practically, for most of us, radio communication is limited. CB sets have only 23 channels, and some of them are for special use or emergencies. There are two ship-to-shore channels for calls home. That only leaves a few channels for the fleet, so you have to wait for somebody to get off the air if you want to talk to a friend.

The first few trips, the thing that surprises me most besides the constant motion is what the salt air does to my face. After two days out, my face gets so stiff and tight I can't smile or make any sudden changes in expression. At the end of the day, it feels great to wash your face. But on good days, after landing 50 or 60 fish, we're too tired to do anything but eat and fall into bed.

We do well the first part of the season. The fish are running close in, and we go out for the day and come back in evenings. The only trouble with fishing with Rudy is that he has discovered there is more to life than fishing. Rudy looks a lot like an aging Willie Nelson, and has more in common with him than his looks. He likes to party and enjoys people. He finds a lot in common with the non-acquisitive musicians and artists that are moving into Mendocino, and spends a lot of evenings there in the bars and coffee houses enjoying their companionship. He will say, "I think it's going to blow tomorrow." We miss some good fishing, but he is ready to go again when the money gets low.

Rudy is unique among the fishermen--and the loggers too--in his favorable response to the area's growing infusion of "hippies." Most natives have no use for them, and consider them bums. Rudy is ahead of his time. He's genuinely interested in their ideas and culture (including pot). He's open minded and receptive to new experiences. He has already rejected materialism for himself, so he has more common ground with them than with most locals.

There are some exceptional musicians moving into the hills around Mendocino, where they like being anonymous. Kris Kristofferson and Rita Coolidge live near Compche, where there is nothing but a gas station and a little store. You can go into a little bar in Mendocino, and Rita Coolidge might be singing there, incognito, just for fun. Sometimes Booker T. Jones is there playing drums. Rudy and the other locals in the bar wouldn't know who they were if they used their famous names, but they know good music when they hear it, and the place is jumping on weekends.

Later in the season we have to go farther out for the fish and we stay out a couple of days at a time. I like the adventure of sleeping on the boat. It's like the most rustic camping. We seldom eat a meal when we're out. It takes a lot to get Rudy's little stove hot enough to boil water. It's a small wood stove and he carries Presto Log chips to burn in it. We have to run ourselves out of the cabin with the heat before it will get hot enough to cook anything. Usually it isn't worth the trouble. We are always eating dill pickles, crackers, salami, cheese, and drinking cups of Gallo Hearty Burgundy. When we come in we look forward to hot meals and comfortable beds.

I've had some experiences on those trips that I wouldn't trade for any amount of comfort. One day I was standing on deck and Rudy said, "Hey, Pat, lift your feet. Here comes a torpedo." I looked in the water and saw one coming. Then I saw half a dozen. They were traveling underwater at amazing speed, heading straight for the boat. Just before they hit the bow, they dipped under the boat, just missing us. Then they were gone, and Rudy was laughing.

"What the hell was that?"

"White dolphins. Japanese dolphins. They're just playing. Do that all the time. First time I saw them I puzzled all day trying to figure out what they were."

They travel in small groups, and speed along in a perfectly straight line; it looks like a chalk line. I never saw a torpedo before except in the movies; I thought it was one.

Rudy will correctly predict the behavior of the whales, sharks, sea lions, and even the birds. He knows things from watching the birds that I have trouble believing. He will see a flock of small birds above the water and tell me how deep the water is where they are and what kind of fish are likely to be there. When we get there, he's right. He says he has always observed that various birds work in certain depths. He uses those observations to get us safely home when the fathometer isn't working, and then I'm a believer. Equipment failures are seldom serious problems for Rudy.

The sea lions are a nuisance, because they will eat the salmon right off your lines. There is nothing more disgusting than pulling up half-eaten salmon. The sea lions know which part they can safely eat, too. If you can't discourage them somehow, one will stay with you all day and eat all the fish.

I was always looking in the wrong place for the sea lion to come up, and finally Rudy mentioned that they always swim counter-clockwise around the boat. He added that if you see them swimming clockwise, there's probably something wrong, some kind of disturbance like an earthquake. After that I could usually anticipate where they would be next, but I probably would never have figured that out on my own.

A sea lion is like a smart dog. They learn fast, and they know what they can get away with. Nobody wanted to hurt them, but on land you can't have wild animals killing your livestock. Fishermen felt the same about sea lions stealing their livelihood, and we used to keep a .22 to shoot at them. It didn't take much to scare them away, because they caught on fast. They wouldn't even put their heads up; they would surface just up to their eyes for a quick glimpse, and then disappear back under. If somebody even intended to shoot them, it wouldn't be easy, but we just wanted them to go away. A few shots near them, and they did.

As familiar as Rudy is with the ocean, he never gets complacent or bored. He's still as fascinated as I am with the unusual things you see once in a while, like the Japanese dolphins or the schools of killer whales, bounding by like aquatic, graceful pandas. They will sometimes be underwater with just their dorsal fins showing; then it looks like white caps coming at us, like a narrow storm.

There is one incredible night out on the ocean when I am glad Rudy is there just to verify it is real. If I were alone, I would have wondered if I had slipped into some other dimension, or maybe dreamed it.

It's a crisp, clear August night. There are more stars visible than I have ever seen before. We're out far enough to drift for the night without hitting the rocks, so there is no noise from straining against an anchor. The ocean is dead calm, smooth as glass. The weather has been good for several weeks, and the water is remarkably clear.

I'm having trouble sleeping because it feels unusual not to have any sound or motion. I step out on deck to look at the stars. For a moment, I feel like I ought to grab something to hold onto.

The mast light is shining on the water where there is a lot of phosphorous, and I can see deep into the water all around the boat, but there is no line visible to mark the separation of sky and water. It seems like we are somewhere up near the moon.

Everything below us is transparent until it fades into darkness. I look up at the stars, and I can see into darkness there too. We seem suspended somewhere in between. I feel like Peter Pan.

I stand there for a long time, in awe. Rudy comes out and watches it too. He has never seen it like this before. Maybe it's like that in the tropics, but on our coast it's rarely calm and clear at the same time. Usually when the ocean is flat calm, there is so much fog you can't see from the cabin to the stern, let alone from the stars to the bottom of the ocean.

The next day Rudy says, "That's what I like about it. Just when I start to think I've seen about everything, there's something different that I'd never see on land."

Whenever there is something unusual, it is fun to be witnessing it with Rudy. First, because if he hasn't seen it before, then you know it's rare, but also because he gets as much pleasure from new experiences as I do. He isn't blase about anything out here. It is still a world of wonder and excitement for him.

One morning we're fishing in the fog and we see a hummingbird circling the boat, lower and lower. We're at least five miles out, and I'm surprised to see him, but Rudy says it's common for land birds to get lost in the fog and land on the boat. The little bird isn't darting around shimmering and flickering at normal speed like they usually do; he's exhausted. He's wary and keeps his distance from us for a while, but he lands on the rail.

Finally, the hummingbird gets so tired he just gives up. He doesn't give a damn who sees him. He flies in the cabin door and lands on a wire to the radio and clings to it. He just hangs on, looking at us, scared. He's gonna die; he doesn't care; he's too tired.

Rudy and I can't let that happen, so we scrounge around to find something to feed him. We consult, and then mix up some sugar water. At first the little guy doesn't want to eat. We have to experiment with a few different containers before we finally get it right. He's terrified, but desperate, so he tries a little sugar water from a jar lid. He likes it, so he tries a little more. He's still pretty scared, but he's being brave and letting us help him because he has no choice.

Rudy likes to stay a safe distance from shore in the fog. He knows it isn't wise to go in closer, but we have to get this little critter close enough to see land, or he's a goner. If he keeps going west and misses Hawaii, his next airport is Japan--almost a quarter of the globe away--and he isn't packing his lunch.

We have to make sure he doesn't fly off on his own again as soon as he gets his strength back, because he's still going to be lost. So we have to put him through some more trauma. We put a box over him as soon as he stops eating, while we pull up the lines and get ready to move out.

Then Rudy carefully figures out where it's safest to venture in in thick fog, where there aren't any rocks offshore, and heads in. The little hummingbird is probably really worried, now that he has the strength to care. Now we're sharing his worries.

As soon as there's a break in the fog and we're close enough to see land, we let him go. He takes off like a rocket, darts out of the cabin, and buzzes straight for land.

We turn around and buzz straight out to sea. We might have lost a few bucks today, but it was worth it.

I learned then, and later rock fishing with him, that what Rudy did in practice differed considerably from what he said his philosophy was. In theory he didn't believe in taking chances. He would say, "I will take a calculated risk, but not a plain risk." There were some things he considered foolhardy. If you asked him, he'd tell you he wouldn't ever do them. If you watched him, he did them all the time. There was no contradiction in that for Rudy. He would just point out that we all do foolish things, or simply agree that he was taking a chance.

Mood has something to do with it, and how you feel. On a beautiful, bright day when there is no sense of foreboding, it doesn't seem like anything could go wrong. On a blustery day, or an overcast, gloomy day, you feel apprehensive and you're less likely to take a chance.

Rock fishing on a bright, clear day we might be fishing close enough to throw a rock on the beach. You're putting everything on the line if you wait until the last minute. You shut the boat off 100 yards from the danger zone, and you fish until you're in it; and then it better start. You don't have a second chance.

Rudy pays cash for everything. He doesn't like to owe money, and he doesn't plan very far ahead. Consequently, he has never owned anything that worked flawlessly all the time--anything that you didn't have to tinker with. He usually allows a little bit for an emergency. He's never had an engine he could really count on. If he did, his "calculated risks" would probably be a lot closer than anybody else's. I always felt safe fishing with him unless he got worried, and I only saw that one time, in heavy weather when we were blown in at Bodega.

For me, fishing with Rudy is probably like winning the first time you pull the handle on a slot machine: you think it's easy to win and you get sucked in. He is so comfortable out there, and even the hard work is upbeat. Every day I see something I've never seen before. You always hear that the commercial fisherman has a life of economic uncertainty, drudgery, and danger. All that is true. But nobody ever mentions that it's so *spectacular* out here. It's hard for me to imagine anything on land that could compete with this.

I have a girlfriend, and I'm sorry to leave her when I go out fishing. I kiss her goodbye and tell her I'm going to miss her. I believe it when I'm saying it, but the truth is--I don't. She's the most important thing in the world to me, on land. When I'm out on the ocean there is no time to think about anything on land. There is so much going on all the time, and it's always such a unique challenge, surviving in a different element, you don't think about bills or worries, or even the good things about home. You're operating on all cylinders all the time, listening for every unusual noise, and then you're exhausted. When I go out of the harbor now, I don't even look back. I know I'm not going to think about anything there until I step off the boat.

I used to see fishermen drive their new cars down to Noyo and leave them parked there to rust until they came back from weeks out albacore fishing. I used to wonder how they could do that. I would think, I'd kill for a car like that, and he lets it rust. Now I can understand it. He isn't thinking about his car, he's thinking about going fishing. Maybe about adventure, maybe the challenge, or maybe just the focus on work, or even escape; whatever fishing is to him.

For me, it's mainly excitement. No matter what your job is on land, you can usually be pretty sure you're going to at least make it through the day. If I knew that for sure, I wouldn't even want to get up in the morning. It's like knowing the end of a movie. I'm confident that I have the drive and determination and, I believe, the resourcefulness, to make it through anything I might have to cope with on any given day. I guess maybe I need the chance to prove that. Fishing is a life that gives you that kind of a challenge all the time.

It's not always life or death. Sometimes it's just a dire need to fix something, without the conventional parts or tools you would have in your garage. Something breaks, and unless you can devise a way to fix it, things are going to be extremely inconvenient or difficult for you. So you get creative, and you feel great when you get it patched together, or invent a workable alternative. On land, you'd go to the parts store or the hardware store, or just go buy another one. Anybody could do it.

I love fishing, but I don't feel much inclined to talk about it when I get home. There isn't that much to tell that someone else could relate to. Even if I'm doing something strictly routine, the surface I'm standing on is rolling around making it more difficult. The motion is exhausting, and when you go to bed it's mesmerizing; it rocks you to sleep. It just isn't like life on land.

When you step back on solid ground, it takes a little while to adjust, like after you take off roller skates and still feel like you have them on. There's even a mental adjustment. You've missed everything that happened while you were gone, and it takes a while to get back in the swing. It's hard to relate to the things people think about on land. For example, when you get home after a harrowing close call coming in the channel, you just don't care much what color the drapes are.

CHAPTER 4

BLOWN IN AT BODEGA

Excitement doesn't describe it: my first confrontation with the sea is electrifying. Everything is fluid; the boat merges with nature. We're part of the air, the wind, the waves as we're tossed around in them. We become spirits of the sea. (For a while we even contemplate becoming part of the sharks.)

Spring 1966

It has been rough all week, and Rudy and I have missed a few days of excellent fishing. Some of the bigger boats have been coming in with great catches, and we're impatient to go out, but the ocean has been too choppy for the past few days.

We're standing out on Todd's point looking at the ocean to see if it's still too rough to go out. Todd's point is on the bluff at the south side of Noyo bridge. It's roughly 60 feet above the breaking surf, and gives you a very good view of the harbor and what the conditions are farther out. There are dirt roads around it from fishermen going up to check out conditions, and from the high schoolers, who use it as a lover's lane. There is no conflict; the kids are usually cleared out by one or two a.m., and the fishermen start arriving about three.

Just as I say I guess nobody is going out, Rudy says Charlie Jones is going under the bridge right now. I look down the bluff and, sure enough, the Devilfish is plowing through the breakers, heading out. That's good enough for Rudy, and he motions for me to get in the van. We're going fishing.

It's easy to go out in this kind of a sea, heading straight into the breakers. All it takes is timing: as soon as a wave passes under you, you speed up to make some headway, and ease off before you hit the next one. You aim for a low spot in the oncoming wave, and speed up when it passes under you. Coming in is the dangerous part, with the breakers behind you trying to dash you on the rocks.

We don't plan on coming in until the conditions are greatly improved. We have fuel and ice enough for about a week. The storm broke a day or two ago, so it should be improving soon, though you can't always tell how rough the ocean will be. Sometimes it stays rough long after a storm. It can be clear with very little wind, and waves will still be breaking over the jetty. It's a gamble when we can get back in here, but we've been waiting around long enough; three days is a long time in the best part of salmon season.

I'm excited about the prospect of making some money. I have no fear at all. As long as Rudy isn't worried, I think it must be okay; I'd follow him anywhere. The fish are running now down off Bodega.

When we get out of Noyo far enough to turn south, I start to experience first-hand the main weakness of a narrow boat in choppy following seas. I wonder if Rudy knows what we're getting into, and at first he doesn't seem concerned. An hour later when we're about off Mendocino, the swells start getting bigger and the boat is broaching down them bad enough to concern Rudy. Now I start to get a little tense.

The Driftwood is a "double ender", the same shape in the stern as the bow, and it resembles a canoe. It's so narrow, you can practically jump from the port to the starboard rail. It is solidly built, but its narrow beam and low freeboard are designed for moderate seas. A boat that narrow will broach badly in anything very wild. That means going sideways down a swell, instead of bow-in. You can get turned sideways in the trough and knocked down by the next breaker.

Rudy is proud of his boat because it is well built and seaworthy, but he doesn't have any illusions about it. He knows its shortcomings, and this is one of them: it will broach in a rough sea.

The weather gets worse as we head south. From the point, it had looked like it was clearing. We thought the rough water was from the storm that was about over, and we expected it to get gradually better. Instead it's suddenly worse. It doesn't take Rudy long to figure out that this is a building sea, not a sea that is tapering off. He can watch the behavior of the wind and the swells and tell in a few minutes what most people wouldn't be sure of for hours. He makes his prediction from watching the size of the swells, their distance apart, and the direction they're coming from. He can pick up slight differences I can't even perceive, and he'll say the swells are getting closer together and more steep. Pretty soon he says this is a new storm, not the remnants of the storm that passed.

When it clouds over and starts raining, it's clear to me too that this is a new storm. The weather reports had predicted it a lot farther north.

Rudy is listening to the boat for unusual noises, paying attention to which way the boat is leaning on every swell, and watching the water for big swells. He is normally very relaxed. Now he's paying a lot of attention to the weather reports on the radio, and more than usual attention to everything else.

It's a new experience for me, being out when it's this rough. There are a lot of white caps, and we're quartering downhill in about ten-foot swells. If you don't like roller coasters, you get a little tired of it. Exhausted, too, because all your strength goes into keeping yourself upright.

I'm steering, and it's a lot of work for the limited benefit. You get so caught up in steering rapidly to point the boat straight down the next swell that you forget you have the rudder at full lock. As you rise on a swell with the boat almost motionless, you forget where center was. Where's the rudder? There is great anticipation before the boat starts smoking down the next swell to see if you have guessed correctly, or have to frantically spin the wheel five full revolutions in the opposite direction.

The boat is also changing position as it rises on each new swell, leaving you to guess which rail you will bury this time: port or starboard. Exhausting, mentally and physically. You're always playing catch up.

Rudy is keeping me distracted by pretending to teach me to steer in heavy weather. He'll say, "You turned a little too far to the left on that one. See how it broached? Next time take it just about a half-turn less to the left."

I listen carefully, and even start counting the turns from right rudder to left rudder, trying to duplicate the turns when I get the best position down a wave. Rudy says, "Yeah, that's good. You got it now." Down the next wave it broaches, and we're standing on the side of the cabin. Then it dawns on me: this is a hell of a time to be practicing. I tell him I think maybe he'd better take the wheel. I could get us in trouble; I've never done this before.

"No, you're doing fine. To tell you the truth, there isn't any right way to steer in this kind of a sea. It's pretty much luck. I couldn't hold it any better. Boat's too narrow. But we'll make it. Just keep it as slow as you can."

By now we know we're going in at Bodega Bay. It's too rough to fish, and it's getting worse. It will take us about four hours to get to Bodega, and there's no point big enough for shelter between here and there. We don't want to try to get back into Noyo. I tell him I think I'll feel better if he steers.

"Hold onto it for a little while and I'll go see if I can catch us a few fish on the way in. Just keep on this heading and go as slow as you can. Don't get in too close, and we might be able to do some good."

Waves are breaking over the cabin periodically. I think he's joking, but Rudy is putting on his boots and oilskins and even his hat. "You can't stay out there. Look at it. The deck is awash most of the time. I can't do any better than this."

"I've seen worse. I've never gone overboard yet. I'll tie on a rope. You look out once in a while."

I'm thinking we don't need money that bad. Rudy says we're going to want a few beers in Bodega. No telling how long we'll be there. This looks like it could keep up for quite a while. We could get pretty lean. Neither one of us has more than a couple of dollars. There isn't much use for money out here, and we don't carry much.

We do carry some, because there is a use for it if we get hungry enough to fire up the stove enough to boil water. If we're close in, we will pull up someone's crab pot and take out 4 or 5 crabs. Then we put some money and some fresh bait in the bait jar, usually a Mason jar with some holes punched in the lid, and throw it in the crab pot and put it back in the water. Then we cook up a couple of crabs and eat them. Somebody will usually see you, but that's not why you do it; it's just a good will gesture. If there's an octopus in the crab pot that's bad news for the crab fisherman, and we keep it. He'd rather have you take it out and sell it; it's not worth nearly what it can eat in crab.

Rudy opens the cabin door and I shudder at the blast of wind. It's blowing pretty good. He can hardly close it, and he holds onto everything there is to hold onto to get to the stern. He's bathed in spray most of the time, and I can't see him clearly, but I can glimpse his bright yellow oilskins. He's got both poles down, and four lines in the water.

I think he's crazy to be out there fishing, with spray coming over the cabin and the boat tossing like a kayak. I feel abandoned, and like everything depends on me. I don't expect him to stay on board, and I don't know how I'm going to rescue him without sealing our mutual doom if I leave the wheel. I'm sure I'll never want a beer that bad. I concentrate on steering the best I can. When the boat rights itself from tipping sideways, I glance back and see if Rudy is still there. He always is.

He fishes for about three hours. He isn't greedy. When he catches one, he packs it up. It's a nice big king, over 20 pounds. I watch him gaff it, leaning over the rail, and then I see green water splash over him and for a while he's obliterated in spray. Then I see the bright yellow again, and Rudy turns toward me and grins, holding up the salmon. That will bring at least twenty dollars. He doesn't waste any time getting the gear in; then he is back in the cabin.

"You're getting in too close. We won't catch anything now." He sounds just a bit annoyed. I've been steering the most comfortable course down each swell, rather than the riskier quartering of each swell, which would have maintained our distance from the beach. But Rudy would have been happy to stay on the roller coaster all the way to Bodega. He isn't mad at me, just irritated with my caution and inexperience. He understands I'm scared, but that's not the way he would have done it.

The greatest frustration for the experienced seaman is that he can't do everything himself. He could have taken the helm and kept us out far enough to catch some fish, or he could have fished on that bucking boat in the spray, because he knew the gear as well by feel as by sight. But he couldn't do both. He was probably out there swearing at my trial and error steering, but he never let on. Since I had to do it, I guess he didn't want to destroy my confidence.

Rudy is always thankful for whatever he gets, and isn't given to complaining. He wouldn't expect an experienced seaman to fish for 15 percent of our small catch, and I think he is fairly well pleased to have found an enthusiastic kid who at least isn't a coward. Once he's in the cabin and grabs a cup of red wine for each of us, he's pretty enthusiastic over that salmon.

We're about an hour from Bodega Bay, and we still have some excitement to look forward to before we are behind the point and into shelter. Bodega Head sticks out a long way. You can be 30 miles off the Golden Gate and be staring at Bodega Head, due north. It's almost as far west as the Farallones. The wind never stops blowing there. It blows so hard, and so constant, that trees or grass won't even grow on the point. Fishermen often refer to it as "Blowdega."

We have to go around that point, and the swells are getting bigger. Behind us and to the west the sky is getting black, and it's mid-afternoon. Rudy takes the wheel, and half the time he's standing on the wall of the cabin to steer. I'm getting bruised all over from getting thrown around the cabin, but I manage to pour us another cup of wine.

Rudy says it's never quite as scary if you laugh about it, and then he laughs. The boat is laying on its side, and we're spilling more wine than we're drinking. This isn't a particularly bad storm, but it's right there at the limits of what this narrow-beamed boat can handle. I can tell that from Rudy's expression. Every time it rolls on its side, the motor dies. He jokes about it, but his demeanor is different. You can see it; not fear, but a seriousness that wasn't there before. We're thinking, if we don't get that sucker started in thirty seconds, we're dead. The boat will be broken into a thousand pieces, and we'll be shark bait. There's an intensity that people on land don't experience very often, except in a few dangerous jobs.

If you're in peril it's some comfort to know exactly how much and what kind. You like to know how scared you ought to be. That's probably because you want to temper it if there's any justification at all. So I'm calculating. What we're getting is only a little worse than what we've already survived. The broaching is a little hairy, but the boat is likely to keep behaving about the same way. Then we're on our side, and my logic gives way to a brief moment of terror. But it's apprehension, more than fear.

Each time we find ourselves standing on the cabin wall, we both figure the next one will put us over, but nobody says anything like that. Even I know that, novice that I am. You never say, "I don't think we're going to make it," because you probably will--if you don't start thinking like that.

We continue to scramble up and down the walls, drinking red wine and laughing like hell. We listen to the radio, and talk about how long we might be stuck in Bodega. Then Rudy says, "We ought to be getting close to that buoy." I stick my head outside and hear, "CLANG.....CLANG.....CLANG." Rudy's instincts once again amaze me. The bell buoy is right there, and he couldn't possibly have heard it with the cabin door closed.

As soon as we get inside the point, the wind dies down and the size of the swells decreases. The tension is gone. Now we know we're going to make it. Rudy takes the wheel to navigate the narrow channel, which has posts to mark safe depth. The harbor looks huge, but most of it is mud flats about two feet deep. The posts are about 100 yards apart, far enough to get lost between them when it's foggy or stormy. Rudy knows about where they are, so I'm glad he is steering. It's a long way in--about three miles from the breakwater to the docks.

This isn't the first time I've had a close call. I've done some challenging driving in cars and motorcycles for excitement. The difference is, I was always in control of the element of danger. It's one thing to tempt the fates when you're setting the limits. This time it was forces of nature completely outside my control. I learned something about myself, and about Rudy, from the way we weathered it, and even something about his boat. I'm not disappointed in any of them.

I notice over the next few months that this experience changed me in ways that I wouldn't have expected. For one thing, I am more relaxed and less inclined to react strongly to minor provocations on land. Most things I used to get upset about seem less important to me now, in contrast with the life-or-death perspective there is on so many things at sea.

When we get into Bodega Bay, the whole Noyo fleet is there. In fact, it looks like every boat on the coast is in at Bodega. We have trouble finding a place to tie up. The bar is really hopping, full of raucous fishermen. For as long as the storm lasts, it will be filled with bored fishermen.

Rudy sells the salmon and gives me half the money, $12.50. I'm only supposed to get fifteen percent, but Rudy is generous because there isn't much to split. Now we have beer money. We don't need more money than that, because most of our necessities are provided for. We sleep on our boats, and have food on them if we run out of cash. There are showers for fishermen above the fish house (which is what we call the processing plant).

Nobody likes being blown in, because you can't make any money. I'm cheerful about it because it's a chance for me to get acquainted with the fishermen and see some of the bigger boats. The home ports are lettered on the stern, and there are boats here from Sausalito, San Francisco, Albion, and even Eureka and Crescent City. It looks like a fishermen's convention. It's the closest thing there is to one. About the only time fishermen socialize is on the radio, or when they are all blown in somewhere.

We spend most of our time sitting around in the bar at The Tides, drinking beer (or in my case, Coke, since I'm underage). The Tides has become a popular place for tourists, because there's a good restaurant and it's right beside the dock. You can look out the dining room windows and watch the boats come in the channel and watch the sea lions and sea gulls around the docks. But the bar caters to fishermen. It's separated from the dining room by windows. At the dinner hour there's some mixing of tourists and locals and fishermen, but they don't care if the fishermen sit there all day. If there's room for the tourists, they can come in too; but the management isn't going to kick out fishermen to make room for them.

There's a dress code on the north coast of California that nobody enforces but everybody adopts: sweatshirts and jeans. All year the temperature seldom gets much below 50 degrees, or much above 70, day or night. It's always a little brisk except on rare summer afternoons when the temperature soars above 70 degrees Fahrenheit, and all the natives think they are dying from the heat. Most of the time there's a slight chill, and nothing feels better than a sweatshirt. For variation you might see a flannel shirt or a sweater, but always denim jeans. That's how the natives and fishermen dress, even to go out to dinner on the wharf, and anybody out of uniform looks overdressed, and is probably a tourist.

There is a town of Bodega, but it's down the highway and inland a few miles from Bodega Bay, so it's not walking distance. It's not a very big town, and there isn't much there but a church and a gas station and a few stores. But at the docks where we are, there's nothing but The Tides bar and restaurant, a gas station and a little gift shop.

The fishermen have nothing to do but answer my questions, so I pick up a lot of information that the rest of them already know. When there's a lull, I'll ask them something about albacore fishing or crabbing--things about other kinds of fishing besides salmon, which is all I've done--and they might start arguing or contradicting each other. I learn more than if I just got one person's opinion.

An innocent question about salmon fishing starts a debate between a "bait fisherman" and a "junk fisherman"--which is what they call someone who uses lures (hardware) instead of herring or other fresh bait. They don't expect to convert each other; each of them does extremely well using his preferred method. They're just passing the time, but it's enlightening to me to hear the points in favor of one or the other. Noyo's two top highliners are one of each; Killer Willie is a junk fisherman, and Carl Youngdahl is a bait fisherman. I guess that proves it isn't the bait that determines success.

One of the fish dealers keeps an old clunker car here for the fishermen to use that has never been washed, and has so many dents it looks like it has been deliberately battered with a hammer, definitely the victim of more than normal wear and tear. Anybody can borrow it, but Rudy warns me that you will be labeled an inconsiderate s.o.b. forever if you take it to the grocery store without packing it full of anybody who wants to go. A capacity crowd always does, because even the Bodega grocery store is a slight change of scene. So there is no thought of going for a ride to break the monotony; it just wouldn't be worth it. It's raining, so walking is out too.

Three of the most successful fishermen are among the most common topics at the bar when they aren't around, because their success makes them celebrities. Everybody is interested in hearing anything about them. Their fishing methods are all entirely different. I learn what their fellow fishermen think they know about them.

According to them, Joe Silveira is efficient and meticulous, and appears to expend no unnecessary effort. He has a Makela brothers boat, and keeps it immaculate. Joe is a bait fisherman. He keeps a moderate number of lines in the water, and once he decides on the most likely place to catch fish, he usually stays in the same general area. He will pick up and move only if he isn't catching fish.

Killer Willie, on the other hand, will run all over the ocean until he finds great fishing. He will keep moving until he does. He doesn't keep trying different lures; he lets his boat and engine do the work. He has the fastest boat around, and he doesn't pamper his engine like most of the other fishermen do. His reputation is enhanced by the way he sounds on the radio. When he keys the mike you know it's him, because you can hear his diesel engine screamin' in the background. I've heard him, and that's true. He runs it wide open all the time; optimum rpm for it is 1800, and he runs his at 2300. That's like keeping your car in second on the freeway and holding it at full throttle. That engine is supposed to self-destruct at around 2100, but it hasn't yet.

Willie takes depreciation literally; he pushes his boat and engine to the limit, and replaces them when they wear out. Most of the other fishermen don't think that way. They're thinking, Willie's never gonna get 15 years out of that engine. Willie is thinking, so many dollars per mile--I can afford to lose a motor if it makes me enough money to be worth it. He's not abusing it, he's using it up.

He has the most versatile boat he could get, so he can jump on whatever is booming. His boat can be outfitted for salmon and albacore, crab, or bottom fish. He's always first to have the latest new equipment. He gets a new boat every 5 years or so because of the loan and tax advantages, but he never gets a bigger boat--just a better one with all the new gadgets.

I remember Willie from unloading boats for Tony. Willie comes across personally as a good-natured, happy-go-lucky guy, never seeming to be serious. He always has a smile, and you would never guess him to be so competitive. He's got much more of a business mind than he lets on, and he obviously enjoys being the best. What I find so remarkable about him is that he couldn't have learned any of this from his dad, or from any of the other guys at the river, because he doesn't do anything the way they do. He must have figured it all out for himself. He acts like he's just having a screaming good time out there and succeeds by accident. But I don't think so.

The others said that Carl Youngdahl seems to work consistently harder at fishing than anybody else, but it pays off for him. He fishes by himself on a 40-foot boat, which is difficult and gets their respect. He goes out earlier, stays out later, and keeps more lines in the water than anybody else. He constantly changes the spoons to different colors until he finds what will work best. It's a lot of work to keep running the lines up and down, checking them and changing the lures. They say that on a 10-fish day for everybody else, Joe or Willie won't usually do much better; but on a 10-fish day, Youngdahl will often come in with a hundred.

Youngdahl fished with his uncle and took over the boat when his uncle retired. His uncle bought his Makela brothers boat from another fisherman who had it built. It was because of him that they almost changed the open-door policy that they had for 40 years. He was there all the time while they were building his boat. He had them put in twice as many ribs as the design called for; it has so much wood in it, they practically rebuilt the log it came from. He supervised every step of the boat's construction and insisted on every minor improvement he could think of to strengthen the boat. It took so much extra time and material, they lost money on it.

The Makela brothers were meticulous by anybody's standards; they built legendary wooden boats, and even selected and cut the timber themselves. They followed the principle that it's always the owner's boat. Many owners even worked on their boats along with Fred and Nick Makela, and most were quite involved in the fitting out and painting. But the Sea Wolf's owner severely tested their traditional mode of operating and their open door policy.

I'm enjoying the stories about the fishermen I've seen all my life from a distance as I watched them unload the boats. I already know who most of the highliners are, and which ones don't ever do very well. It's interesting to see how their traits carry over, even in trips to the grocery store.

Youngdahl doesn't go often. When he does, he checks out every item, down to the smallest purchase, comparing brands and prices on what little selection there is. He will consider something for maybe five minutes, then decide he can get along without it. With him, it's a big deal buying a box of crackers.

Joe is just the opposite. Going with him is simple. He never goes unless he has a good reason. He knows exactly what he wants--maybe a can of pepper, some toothpaste, a can of tomatoes--and buys it. Then he's ready to go back. You can't sidetrack him.

Killer Willie will go just to look around. He's an explorer, and he always will find something interesting. He'll buy something he hasn't tried before, but it doesn't take him long. He's always ready to move on ahead of everybody else.

Back in the bar we hear stories about "lowliners" too, but they aren't called that. I guess they could be called losers, but nobody is that unkind. There are just some fishermen who have no luck at all catching fish. One of them was a dentist who decided he wanted to fish instead. He has an expensive boat and all the best equipment. He seems to do everything right, but he can be in the middle of a fleet where everybody around him is pulling them in, and he will hardly catch a fish. The other fishermen have several theories about what might be wrong. The most common is that there must be some kind of noise coming from the boat, maybe a bearing, that spooks the fish.

One of the fishermen tells me a story of how the boat "Proudfoot" got that name. It belongs to one of the highliners who came back to fishing after working in the sawmill for 20 years. The sawmill managers hired a company of efficiency experts called Proudfoot, and in their report they said the company didn't need that man's job. Before they could reassign him to some other position, or even discuss it, he quit and got a fishing boat. He named it Proudfoot, and has been fishing ever since. Most of the guys think he was looking for a reason to quit. Somebody probably could have said boo to him any time in the last 20 years, and he would have been back fishing.

I know most of the fishermen around my age, because we went to school together. Sam Connors was a few years ahead of me, but his wife and my girlfriend are good friends, so I usually join him and Louie, a crewman with him on his uncle's boat, when we're in the bar. He gives me a few fishing tips, but mostly we talk about racing dirt bikes, and the clunker cars we've owned. We're kids reminiscing about the recent "old days". I have no doubt that Sam will be fishing all his life, but it turns out that it's not in the cards for him. That bizarre saga unfolds later.

Every day we sit around the bar for a while, walk around the small dock area, and maybe do some maintenance on our boat. Then one of the Italian or Portuguese fishermen invites us all for dinner on his boat. The crowd has thinned out after the first day or two, because a lot of the ones from nearby ports, like Fort

Bragg, called their families to pick them up. They are sitting it out at home until the weather clears.

The second night we're in, Joe Silveira bakes a huge salmon with a tomato sauce and parsley, and serves a big salad, French bread and spaghetti with it. He's a great cook, but it's the salmon that impresses me the most. We rarely eat salmon, even though we all like it. It's like eating money right out of your wallet.

The boat interests me more than the dinner. It's the first time I've been on a Makela brothers boat. Joe has had the Maria about five years, but it looks new. Every time it has a hint of dry rot or fungus, he has it taken out of the water and inspected. The Makela brothers repair it if they find anything wrong; he wouldn't consider letting anyone else do the repairs.

Most of the fishermen keep their boats in fairly decent repair, but inside most of them look like a combination workshop-garage (which they are); Rudy's looks like a hamster cage. Joe's is immaculate. He keeps the deck mopped and the varnished rails shined. You wipe your feet before you step aboard the Maria, like you would entering somebody's living room.

You might expect to see a maid, if you didn't know that no woman has ever set foot on this boat, not even in port. Joe is devoted to his wife and daughter. They can have anything they want: trips, cars, clothes, they have a beautiful home; but they have never been allowed on this boat, even to look at it. They wouldn't even ask. It's bad luck.

Joe's isn't the only boat at Noyo that has never had a woman on it. This is one of the strongest superstitions among the Portuguese and Italian fishermen, and one that many of the others subscribe to. The only time a woman can safely be on a boat is at the time it's first launched. Superstition is a part of sea lore that has a mysterious power over fishermen, whether they admit to it or not. All fishermen are superstitious, and if you're around them long enough, you are too. You don't know what your luck depends on, and if there's some taboo or other that somebody thinks it is, well, maybe you'd better not risk it. I know it's irrational, but if I had a boat I'm not sure what I'd do if a woman asked to go aboard.

There are not many women fishing at Noyo, but there is one who has her own salmon boat. She does well, and keeps a crewman or two. There are a few women who fish with their husbands. Those men obviously disregard the superstition, but it's ingrained in the culture at Noyo for many. It's one of those die-hard traditions that might be followed by some for ulterior motives, but for others it's as strong as their religion. It's probably the reason that fishing has remained one of the few careers that is almost exclusively male.

There might be some practical reasons the superstition has endured. Most small salmon boats don't have a room with porcelain fixtures. For two men on a boat, the waist-high gaff hatch in the stern provides as much privacy as they need. If a bucket with a rope tied on (to retrieve some water) and a toilet seat for it are stowed in the gaff hatch, it's almost like home, and you have an incredible view. You just time it so it doesn't conflict with the fishing schedule. When you don't need a place to sit down, arrangements are even more informal. A woman's presence on the boat could complicate this. It's a convenient superstition. But a Makela brothers boat is equipped with a head, and many other conveniences, so Joe is honoring tradition or superstition.

Joe worked a long time for that boat, and he's very proud of it. The Maria is without question the best kept boat at Noyo. But it's his nature to be meticulous and take good care of things. The others said he kept his old Monterey Clipper the same way.

After dinner, I get one of the crew members to show me around the boat. The equipment in the wheel house reminds me of the studio at the local radio station; he must have everything on the market. The crewman is proud of it; he says all the electronic equipment is top of the line. I wonder how he'd feel about Rudy's equipment.

This is the most solid, beautifully built boat I've ever seen. I've heard about Makela brothers boats all my life, because this is another realm, besides disaster, where the fishing and lumber communities come together. My dad and my uncle have told me all about these boats, from the lumberman's perspective, and I can appreciate this one because I know what goes into building one. They are the Steinway of wooden boats on this coast, according to the local fishermen and the loggers.

They start with 3" x 3" steam-bent oak frames on 12-inch centers for the ribs. Then they are double-planked with 2-inch thick planking outside, and 2-inch ceiling on the interior (inner skin). They use Douglas fir heart with no knots. It can take years to gather the wood for one of these boats. The Makela brothers always have the lumber company scouting for the perfect tree, and sometimes they have to go out in the woods and find one themselves. Their specifications call for virgin (first growth) north slope Douglas fir. That's the slowest growing with the most consistent growth rings. It also has to be perfectly straight grained.

My dad says they have to scout the timber because the lumber company would have to go through 10 units of lumber (10,000 board feet) to find one stick suitable for building a Makela brothers boat. He thinks there's a question of whether that much quality is absolutely necessary. Makela brothers would discard a piece of wood for imperfections so minor it was incomprehensible to my dad. For example, for a tight pin knot. "There's no reason you can't have one through the wood at a 45 degree angle; a sound knot is part of the growth of a piece of wood; it isn't going to fall out." Still, my dad was impressed with their standard of perfection.

When the tree is spotted, the Makela brothers buy the tree standing ("on the stump") and take responsibility for getting it down and cut up the way they want it. They have someone fall it, and it might take two or three days to lay a bed for it to make sure it doesn't break up. There is more danger of its breaking than other trees because of the perfectly straight grain.

Then they cut it up themselves with an Alaskan mill (a portable chain sawmill). They cut it into big timbers, and haul the timbers to their shop. The timbers are cut into planks with an antique band saw, reportedly by eye. The people who have watched them say they never saw them use a guide of any kind. That's another thing my dad and my uncle used to marvel over.

The original plans they use are Ed Monk designs. Wooden boats are always built to a standard plan and a proven design, at least from the water line down. Makela brothers boats vary in length, but they are basically the same; you know them immediately if you have ever seen one.

The Makela brothers instill confidence as boat builders, because they fish with the first commercial boat they built, the Condor. They usually fish for six months of the year, and build and repair boats the other six.

It normally takes two and a half years for them to complete a 55-foot boat like the Maria. There is always a waiting list to get a Makela brothers boat built. At a time when you can buy the best house in Fort Bragg for $50,000, a Makela brothers boat sells for $160,000. But then, to a fisherman, a house is nothing but a poorly built boat.

We have dinner on several of the other big boats. When we go back to ours, it's starting to seem as rustic to me as a dugout canoe. To Rudy, the big boats seem like too much work and responsibility, but I'm interested in making more money. I don't mind working hard, and I can't wait to get on a bigger boat and start learning the equipment, and working my way up to one like the Maria.

The second day we're in Bodega, a Fort Bragg boat comes in from fishing south of here. The skipper had picked up a new crewman in San Francisco--probably a relative who wanted a job. It was his first time out, and his last; he was sick all the way. When he got to Bodega he took a bus back to San Francisco, saying goodbye to fishing forever, and leaving the skipper by himself on a boat too big for one man to operate alone. They're chuckling about it in the bar. This is not an uncommon occurrence. For many, one day on the Pacific is enough.

When I hear about it, I think immediately that it might be my chance to get on a bigger boat. I mention it to Rudy and he says maybe we better go look at the boat before I talk to the skipper. Rudy doesn't say anything to try to discourage me. He can handle his boat by himself, and it isn't his nature to try to influence anyone else in their decisions.

We look over the St. Jude, and I can tell the skipper isn't prosperous by the shape the boat is in. Rudy looks it over carefully and gives me his opinion: "She doesn't look like much, but she's seaworthy. That's a good design, even by today's standards. The trouble is, she's poorly built. But it looks like she's taken a lot, and probably will stand a lot more."

Rudy can tell by looking that it was poorly executed by the builder, but even I can tell that the poor workmanship was compounded by years of neglect and gradual decay. It looked good from a distance, but up close we can see that the timbers are rotten and the deck beams are all cracked. Even in this calm anchorage, the boat creaks and moans when it rolls against the anchor.

The one negative thing Rudy says is, "I think I'd worry more about the skipper than the boat. I've heard he's had a lot of bad luck."

When I ask what kind of bad luck, Rudy says he has lost a boat or two--at least one--but he doesn't remember the details. "But that doesn't necessarily mean he's a bad skipper. That can happen to anybody. I've been real lucky."

That night we're invited to dinner on a Monterey Clipper from Sausalito. Everybody calls them the "mosquito fleet" because a group of them fish together. They're small boats and, unlike the rag-tag Noyo fleet, which ranges from Rudy's Driftwood to the "Great Pumpkin", they are all identical. There's another fleet of them that fishes out of San Francisco. Rudy is intrigued with those boats, and makes the comment that he never did hear of one of these ever flippin' over. That sparks a discussion about the relative merits of various kinds of boats, to which I can't contribute any insights, but certainly earn my place as a rapt listener.

The skipper has been through some rough weather in his Monterey Clipper, and feels pretty secure in it. He says it's not too good buckin' into it, but it's better than anything else broadside; it doesn't roll much. They agree that taking it broadside is what you usually worry about. Rudy knows something about them, and tells the others that the planks are beveled, not caulked, and that it's built to a Phoenician pattern. They talk about the small house being less for a wave to catch, and what a good design it is for staying alive in the water when it kicks up. "The sea can't get a grip on 'em."

I guess nobody there has a boat with a flying bridge, because those really get trashed. Some of the old fishing boats have them, and it's like driving a car from the center of the front seat. You can't see well out the sides, but you're higher than anything else so you can easily see the docks. The veterans there agree they are handy for maneuvering in the harbor, but that's about all. One says they can be a help when albacore fishing, because you can see a school from a long distance if they're feeding on squid at the surface. You see the water surface all choppy. Everything else you're looking for is so far below the surface, a little more height doesn't help. They all think that even for albacore, it isn't worth the added risk of being a bigger target for high seas.

I'd like to ask them why boats are never an even 30, 40, or 50 feet; they're always 32, 55 or 56--some unusual number. I don't, because I think it's probably a dumb question. I never do find out.

At Noyo you see a lot of innovation in boats. Everything from a whaler with a home-made square cabin to a converted Navy P-T boat is employed in commercial fishing. They say the couple with the P-T boat winters in Acapulco with it. It's 85 feet long and has four Detroit diesels. It can go 30 knots, which is quite a sight. There's a large roostertail of water flying behind the boat, and it goes up on a crest like a speedboat. Rudy says he wouldn't like to pay their fuel bill, and we all laugh. Somebody says they have a complete machine shop on the boat, a water maker, and a weather machine. On the rails where the depth charges used to be, they have two Hondas, one on each side, with sailcloth covers. Those are for land transportation. I'm thinking the only thing better would be a Ferrari Dino, and a ramp to drive it off. That boat sounds like fun.

After dinner, Rudy and I go to the bar for a drink. I ask him what he thinks about the others' opinions about boats. He says fishermen allow sentiment to influence them. The boat they happen to have is the ideal boat. He observes that people are the same way about their dogs. When I ask Rudy to describe what he thinks the ideal boat would be, I find out something I didn't know about him.

"Some of them think fiberglass or steel is best because it's stronger if you go on the rocks. I think wood is best, because you're not supposed to go on the rocks. I like the feel of a wooden boat, and how it rides on the water. A steel boat rides like a tin pan. You have to have a boat you can believe in.

"It should have a deep hull, a strong wheel house, and back-up plates to keep the windows from breaking. Not bow-heavy or top-heavy. It should have a stout vertical stem, and a watertight compartment in the bow; the bulkhead in front of the foc's'le could have an airtight door. I believe a 32-footer would be the most seaworthy. A Westwind Ketch is the most seaworthy boat there is. It will stay up when the ships go down. Not a very high cabin, and the cabin to the rear, not forward, so it will hold bow in with a sea anchor in heavy seas."

It occurs to me that Rudy is not describing a salmon boat. You couldn't have the cabin to the rear, because you need to watch the tops of the poles from the gaff hatch; it would block your view. The boat he's describing isn't for fishing at all; it's what you'd want as the ideal boat for sailing alone around the world. Now I begin to understand why he doesn't take fishing very seriously.

Rudy's hero is Captain Joshua Slocum, the first man to sail alone around the world. Rudy has read a lot about Slocum, and tells me that the Northern Light at Noyo was named for a ship that Slocum had an interest in and once commanded. Slocum described it as the finest American sailing vessel afloat in the 1880s. Even Snug Harbor gets its name from Slocum's sailing days, when Sailor's Snug Harbor was a refuge for retired seamen.

Rudy has one big advantage over Slocum. Before setting off on his world voyage in the Spray, Slocum reported that he spent a season in his new craft fishing on the coast, only to find that he "had not the cunning properly to bait a hook."[1] Rudy's guile for fishing may have shaped his destiny.

The next day the weather is still blustery, but has calmed down quite a bit. The fishermen are getting impatient. It would be better if we could see what the ocean is like, but Bodega Bay is just like Sausalito; it's so far in from the ocean that it can look calm in the harbor and still be screamin' out there. We'll probably pack up a car full and drive up the highway a few miles to get a look at it tomorrow. It's easier to have some patience if you can at least see how bad it is. That's one thing I prefer about Noyo; you can see what the ocean is doing.

---

[1] Slocum, Joshua Sailing Alone Around the World; W. W. Norton & Company, New York, London, 1984; p. 7

I haven't approached the skipper of the St. Jude, but I've been inquiring about him, and he has been inquiring about me. Finally somebody introduces us, and we talk about his predicament and my interest in getting on a bigger boat. I'm pretty confident of getting hired, because a lot of experience obviously wasn't among his criteria when he picked the last crewman. He offers me the job, and I tell him I'll talk to Rudy. I'm pretty sure it won't be a problem for him, and it isn't.

Chapter 5

St. Jude

He that will learn to pray,
let him go to sea.
George Herbert

Spring 1966

When the St. Jude leaves Bodega, I'm on it. If Rudy or the other fishermen had offered any really discouraging information, I probably would still have decided to go on this creaking boat with its uncertain skipper. One of the fishermen did tell me that he had heard that Alex Johnson, skipper of the St. Jude, had lost two boats in the past two seasons. He didn't know any of the details.

I'm too excited with moving up so far on the scale of amenities to be very concerned about safety. It may be surprising that I'm so impressed with what later came to be standard equipment in a class A motor home, but it seems pretty plush on a fishing boat, compared with what I'm used to. We have a full head, a shower, hot and cold running water--not just running by. There's a dinette type dinner table--we can sit down to eat. It even has formica counter tops. This is really modern after the Driftwood.

The size of the pilot house impresses me, too. It's so big, there are two bunks in it, besides the four bunks below. The bulkheads are jammed with equipment: Loran, fathometer, radios, everything except radar, but radar is not too common on boats this size. This boat has a hydraulic anchor winch. I'm going to appreciate that, too.

I like the skipper. He tells me the St. Jude is leased, but doesn't tell me right away what happened to his last boat. Alex is a very pleasant person to work for, but he is as unlike Rudy as anyone I can imagine. We're scarcely out of sight of the harbor when he begins worrying about his exact position, and he never stops being anxious about it for more than a few minutes all the time I fish with him. The only time he is really at ease is when it's crystal clear and we're in sight of land.

When I saw the name on this boat, I thought St. Jude must have been a favored saint, like St. Elmo is the patron saint of sailors. I didn't know, and didn't bother to investigate. I'm not sure now there was a significance beyond remarkable coincidence, but in view of the events of those several months I often look back and wonder if I could have found a warning in that name.

I don't attach much significance to the name of a boat, except that a confident name like "Sea Wolf" can be reassuring. The majority of them at Noyo are named for wives or girlfriends. Besides, Alex didn't name the boat-- he just leased it. Of course, he did pick this boat to lease; maybe the name appealed to him, in view of his history with boats. I don't think much about it, because I don't learn until much later that since the 18th century, St. Jude has been considered the patron saint of desperate causes.

The St. Jude is a little over 50 feet long, and looks like a typical west coast design, similar to a Makela brothers boat, but from a different builder. From a distance it seems to have good lines, but when you get close it becomes apparent that it does not have the strength you would want in a boat for the Pacific northwest.

Boats for use here are built with survivability the first and foremost design consideration, and are very different in design and layout from small east coast fishing boats. The main reason for the design differences is that on the east coast there is usually a convenient harbor to run into whenever you need one. The few harbors in the Pacific northwest are far apart, so the boat has to be able to survive a storm. There are some other reasons for the differences. On the east coast there are a lot of shallows, in and out of the harbors, so the boats have to be designed accordingly.

Most small east coast fishing boats have a flat floor from the back of the cabin to the stern, and the rails are above knee height. They store fish mostly on deck; they can take on more water, and would be unsafe for the west coast. Here, the boats have higher decks that are solid from the bow to the stern, leaving the rails much lower, about shin height. Fish are stowed deep in the boats, with hatches for access. The coaming is about waist high. A west coast fishing boat would be considered overkill on the east coast, except for going out long distances. An east coast boat usually has time to run for port before the waves get high enough that green water comes over the side.

On a Makela brothers boat, the ribs extend above the deck line, forming the bulwarks. The St. Jude has fewer ribs, and they extend only to deck level, more like an east coast design. The bulwarks, or rails, are added on, making for a weak structure from the deck up. That's the reason for all the straining and creaking and groaning Rudy and I noticed with the boat anchored. There's not enough strength amidships where the salmon trolling poles attach to the rails, and the entire boat flexes more than a wooden boat of these proportions should.

This is not a big cause for concern. As Rudy says, the boat looks like it has taken a lot and will probably take a lot more. The greater concern is probably the skipper. He appears cautious; we stay in Bodega a full day after most of the fleet has gone out, before he decides it's safe.

When we finally get out and start fishing, I find that the gear is easy to learn; it's about the same as Rudy's, there are no big differences. For the first few days, I'm really enjoying the new luxuries and being on a bigger boat. Things go pretty well, until the first time we get some fog.

The height of salmon season is the summer. Although we have fog off and on most of the year, the worst foggy season here is also summer. The temperature here, day or night, is usually between 50 and 70 degrees as long as you're off California. Farther north, fishing off Oregon and Washington, it gets colder. It's a lot colder off Alaska, and they have to contend with ice. Here, it gets a little colder than 50 degrees at sea when there's a breeze, but there are no real extremes. We might get frost in the winter about once every five years. We get our best weather in the spring and fall; that's when we get the most frequent clear days. When it's hot inland it's usually foggy on the coast. In the summer, it's foggy about half the time.

Fog is a mixed blessing to fishermen. The fact that it is almost always flat calm when there is heavy fog far outweighs the navigational inconvenience. If you happen to find a hot spot, you can have it all to yourself. No one will see you, then tell a friend over the radio where the fish are, and bring the whole fleet down on top of you. Then you spend more time dodging other boats than landing fish.

Alex has Loran, so you'd think he'd feel secure; but he goes into a state of panic whenever he can't see land. He has to know exactly where he is, and verify it about every 15 minutes. He has no confidence in his own navigational skills or in his equipment, especially his Loran.

Alex is a good navigator. He just doesn't know it. He figures out where he is and he's right, he's fine--as long as it's clear. He goes crazy in the fog. He doesn't believe his Loran, and he has to go see something. He has to know where he is every minute. We're always pulling up all the gear so he can get in closer and find a familiar rock. I'm always afraid he'll find it and get us killed.

I feel sorry for him, because you can tell he is really worried. I can see it in his face. He will look relaxed and confident--as confident as he ever gets. A few minutes later I'll look at him and see that worried frown: he has lost it. He isn't sure he knows exactly where we are. Then we start chasing around to find out. We spend more time doing that than we do fishing. He will tell me what's causing the uncertainty. The last reading he got didn't seem consistent with the ones before.

I get tired of picking up the gear all the time, running around to see where we are, when it doesn't matter. We aren't going to know any better running around all over. If we ran into a road sign that said, "Fort Bragg - 69.7 miles, and you're 15 miles offshore", I don't think it would have mattered. He would have wanted to know what side of the sign we were on. He is really paranoid about knowing where we are--and he never does. That's the sad part. In spite of all that equipment, I think I always have a better idea of where we are than he does.

His ability isn't any less than anybody else's. He just worries about it more. I do too, because of his lack of confidence compared with Rudy. If I were fishing with anybody else, they would have been satisfied if they knew they were either 20 or 25 miles from the harbor. You're preoccupied when you're fishing and you aren't going in. You could get a more accurate fix with the Loran if you really needed it, but there's no point in knowing every minute of every day where you are.

Alex has to know within a mile. If he doesn't know if it's 19 or 20, he is concerned. Enough to stop what he's doing to find out. He is always playing with the Loran. Whenever he gets a reading, there is something wrong with the reading or the Loran. If you're preoccupied with that kind of information, it can take up all your time.

I'm beginning to think you're better off without Loran, because it's not that hard to navigate without it, and you focus on fishing. Rudy had neither Loran nor autopilot. Without landmarks to go by, our tacks were in a zig zag fashion all over the ocean. We knew where we were in relation to home, but that was about all. It never seemed important. When it came time to anchor, we would run in to about 5 to 10 fathoms and anchor.

We knew the coast along this area, of course. During the day we stayed in the depth where we knew there were fish, making long tacks until we got into some fish. Then we would double back and work that area until they disappeared.

Finding your way home was simple. We would run at buoy depth (26 fathoms) while closely watching the compass. There were several variations in the contour of the bottom that were very obvious giveaways to your position when compared to the chart. For instance, one long stretch of sandy beach just north of home ran due north and south, as opposed to northwest and southeast for the rest of that area, that would require you to turn out to stay in 26 fathoms. After ten minutes on this new course, with no change in depth, there was no doubt where you were. At the end of this stretch of beach was a reef. When passing over the reef, your fathometer readings would vary from 15 to 30 fathoms, leveling off right near 26 fathoms on the other side. From that, it was a simple compass heading to the buoy, correcting, if necessary, to stay at the right depth.

After about 30 minutes, you would shut down and listen for the buoy. If you felt you had overestimated your running time and missed the buoy, you just kept going until you could either see or hear the lighthouse and foghorn at Point Cabrillo, about six miles south of the harbor. Then you could try it again from that direction.

We almost always heard the buoy the first time we shut down. That was mostly due to Rudy's skill in dead reckoning navigation, and the knowledge to use what he happened to have. With that kind of introduction to navigating in the fog, I had lots of confidence, and never felt the need to know *exactly* where I was. On one occasion we went four straight days without knowing. We were on top of the fish and doing very well. Our position in relation to them was considered to be the most important problem at hand.

Alex would be better off without Loran, and with a different set of priorities of what was important in navigating this coast in the fog. He had forgotten how to navigate without Loran, if he ever knew, and had become much too dependent on it when it wasn't that reliable on this coast.

Part of Alex's anxiety could be from his having run on the rocks at Point Reyes *because* of a miscalculation. The boat was on auto pilot; he thought they had miles to go. He was sitting at the kitchen table when they ran into the rocks, going full bore. There were three men on the boat, and he was the only survivor. His two crewmen drowned. He was picked up in the water.

When he told me about this, we talked about the reliability of Loran. He said the Loran station was off Bodega Head, and it never did work very well in that area when you got too close to the Loran station. But it was more likely that he relied too heavily on Loran for longitude, when the nearest Loran station to the west was a weak signal from Hawaii. I wasn't sure where all the Loran stations were at this time, but I heard that from fishermen who had them.

Loran measured time differentials of two intersecting ground-based radio signals. The accuracy depended on how the two signals intersected at your particular location. The closer it was to a right angle, the better the fix.

Loran skills varied among the fishermen as much as the equipment. Some fishermen had new units with owner's manuals, and they were diligent and precise about learning to use them properly. Others were using military surplus units of various age and condition, some without owner's manuals, and were applying their precision instruments very imprecisely. Some of them tried to use it with very little knowledge of the technology. Even I could see the futility in that.

Once when Rudy and I were out, he was playing with an old Loran somebody gave him, and asked me, "Pat, how far is it out Sherwood Road to KDAC?" That was the local radio station. Even if I knew it was two or three miles, that wouldn't have been precise enough to get an accurate Loran fix from its signal intersecting with another one, even if he knew its exact distance. It was a joke. But at least Rudy knew he was just playing, not staking his life on it. He was just curious to see how they worked.

I don't know where Alex or his equipment belongs in this varied scale of competence. I'm trying not to second-guess him or be too judgmental, because I haven't had much experience. He's so diligent, he even sleeps in the pilot house when we're out; he only sleeps below when we're in port. It's a lot more comfortable below, because the lower you get in the boat and the nearer the center, the less motion there is. All that vigilance should make me feel secure, but it has just the opposite effect. I never felt insecure with Rudy, and his theory that the thing to do in the fog is stay well out and away from the rocks makes a lot of sense to me.

One evening, a couple of weeks after Alex tells me how he lost his first boat, I learn how he lost his second one--almost by personal experience. We have a very similar close call in the shipping lanes and a huge freighter almost runs us down.

Ships can avoid a fleet easily, but may not always see a single boat. Their radar is fine-tuned, so their radar can sometimes mistake a boat for a whitecap; or vice-versa. It scans the top of the water, so if it's smooth they can pick out a small boat. Because a small wooden boat is such a poor radar target, most of the wooden boats put something metal on their masts so they can be distinguished on radar; even aluminum foil will work. We had a lot of metal on our mast, thanks to what I thought was Alex's paranoia. (Actually, something really was out to get him, if only his own insecurity.)

We are fishing between Point Reyes and the Farallones with a fairly large fleet, in pea soup fog. We're tacking east and west in and out of the shipping lanes (clearly marked on the charts). This was not unusual or especially dangerous if you were careful, used common sense, and watched your fathometer. By comparing fathometer readings with the chart, you can determine your position in and out (east and west) fairly close. Up and down (north and south) was a little more difficult, but not as important. We had Loran and auto pilot, which enables you to make very straight tacks. So if you know where you started, there isn't much excuse for not knowing where you are within a mile or so, and closer than that with accurate Loran readings.

For some reason, Alex seems more nervous than usual. Granted, being in and out of shipping lanes presents special problems that we don't encounter most of the time, except in this area. Where we fish during most of the season, the fishable depth is well inside the shipping lanes. We're in this area now because it's where the salmon are. Alex is very uncomfortable, if not scared to death, but he's hiding it.

Really thick fog does weird things to sight and sound, especially on the ocean. We are running in thick fog, and we hear a ship's horn in the distance. The sound makes my skin tingle, because I can't tell where it's coming from. Alex opens up the engine to full speed and runs about five minutes in another direction, and it's still there. He changes direction again, and runs five or ten more minutes, and it's still there. Then we hear a blast of its horn right behind us, and I jump out of my skin. It's close. Alex changes direction again, and runs five or ten more minutes. After an hour of that, trying to evade it five or six times, we're finally in the clear.

Then we see a slick from their propeller, in a wavy line like a snake. Good thing it's foggy so they can't identify us. They have been trying to avoid us with a thousand foot ship that takes a lot of room to turn, and we have been darting back and forth in front of them.

When our hearts stop pounding, Alex confesses that he lost his last boat when it was run down by a freighter. He was tacking east and west, in and out of the shipping lanes.

He was picked up after becoming entangled in the rigging as the ship passed over him. He was the only survivor; a crewman drowned. It was later determined that the ship had the right of way and he was at fault. The suit for damages to the ship's propeller was dropped when it was found he had no insurance on his boat. I'm pretty clear now on why he's so nervous; and I'm very nervous myself.

It stays foggy for the next couple of weeks and we get very little fishing in. We are not having a good season, even though the fish are here and everybody else is catching them. We spend too much time navigating. At least now I understand why, but it doesn't make me feel any better.

Then one day the inevitable happens. It's very thick fog, and visibility isn't even fifty feet; we can't see from one end of the boat to the other. Sometimes it clears in the afternoon, but today it shows no signs of lifting. Alex is getting very anxious. We're fishing somewhere south of Bodega, a little north of Bolinas, and Alex decides he has to find out exactly where we are. He decides he has to see land. I know this is a big mistake, but he's the skipper. Mutiny crosses my mind, but I reject the idea.

I pull up the lines, and Alex starts heading for shore at moderate speed. As we get closer to shore, I get a feeling of impending doom. In the fog, everything is muted; colors, sounds. Nothing seems quite as real. If you can see the outline of anything, it's vague and you can't quite make it out. You have to be on top of something before you can clearly see it.

I'm thinking we might end up in the water. I'm also thinking how preposterous it is to take this horrendous chance of getting killed or losing your boat, just to ease your mind about where you are, when it doesn't matter anyway. He isn't planning to go in, and we're not near anywhere we could go in, so what's the point? It's more important to Alex to know where he is than it is to be safe, and I am now realizing just how deranged that is.

I'm watching very carefully to see the outline of anything, but I know we're going to be on top of it before I see it. I don't think about putting on a life jacket, because I gave up that idea the first or second time I was out with Rudy. There has to be a life jacket for every person on board, and all the boats comply, even Rudy. But the reality is, they are not going to be much help in most circumstances if you find yourself in the water. If the boat breaks up on the rocks, you're going to get dashed on the rocks too. A life jacket isn't going to save you.

Before I ever went out on the ocean, I thought of a life jacket as a reassuring thing to have. As soon as I went out there, and was out of sight of land and any other boats, I realized the futility of thinking you were likely to be rescued. If you get a chance to use the radio and give your position, someone still would take a long time to get there, and has to find you.

The water temperature where we fish varies with the seasons, but it is always somewhere between 47 and 60 degrees. It's never much above 47 in salmon waters, and only gets up to 60 in the albacore grounds farther out. If you're in water this cold for very long, your body loses the ability to maintain temperature control, and your body temperature will get too low. Most fishermen know the term for this: hypothermia. All of them know the body loses heat much faster in water than in the same volume of air, and they will die within 45 minutes to two hours if they end up in this water.

So you don't have much time to wait for someone to save you.

Survival suits are available, but they cost $800 each. I don't know of any fishing boats here that have them. You would need one of those to live long enough in the water for someone to rescue you, unless they were close enough to see you go in the water.

If you go on the rocks in the fog, it's sudden and you don't have time for a Mayday. Nobody is going to see you in the fog.

Out at sea, the odds are just as bad. The closest planes and helicopters over 100 miles away. In 1961 the Coast Guard replaced Fort Bragg's 83-foot cutter built for the Normandy landing with a new 82-footer with two turbocharged V-12 Cummings diesels. It can do 30 knots, but you could be a long distance from there. Even with a plane or a helicopter, they have to find you. With a search radius of maybe a hundred miles--even if they are searching for you, and have a general idea of where your boat went down--and even if you were lucky enough to be a first priority call with only two of you aboard--the chances of anyone finding little you bobbing around in your life jacket are slim, if not none.

You realize after the first time out that if you're more than a mile from shore, a life jacket would only prolong the inevitable. You're fishing in a remote part of the Pacific northwest, where there isn't anyone handy to rescue you. You see the futility of thinking about it, and you put it out of your mind. It's such a silly little solution for such a monumental problem, you might as well forget it.

You're responsible for yourself. You save yourself, or you die. It's what you always have to think about when you do any dangerous thing. Nobody else is responsible for saving you, and you don't count on it. No fisherman does.

If you had a leak in the boat, you would grab a life jacket and radio for help, hoping that somebody was close enough to pick you up. Especially on a clear day, when they have some chance of finding you.

If another boat is close by, you expect them to help you if they can. Everybody respects the Coast Guard, and is glad they are there to rescue people in distress whenever they can. But all fishermen know they put themselves in danger, and they don't go out expecting that someone will be there to bail them out of trouble. You don't rely on the Coast Guard to tow you in because you forgot to clean your carburetor; you clean it before you go, so you won't get in that situation.

The reality is, most fishermen wouldn't call for help until it was too late. A tough old Italian fisherman would still be trying to fix the problem when the water was up to his knees. He wouldn't call for help unless he was sure the boat was going down. He probably wouldn't put out a Mayday until he was in water up to his waist; then he would think, "I'm out of options totally now; I guess I'd better call somebody." Even then, he would know that everything depended on him; he wouldn't be expecting to be saved.

It isn't exactly humiliating to be rescued; you would appreciate it, but you would really regret having got into the position that it became necessary. I'm sure most fishermen don't think like I do, because I enjoy the excitement of danger and life-threatening risks, and being able to survive them. In my case, I'd probably be a little resentful if the Coast Guard plucked me out of the water. I'd think, I'd like to have found out if I would have survived without you. But that's probably not the way most people think.

Fishermen are very independent, though. They face the dangers, and they don't place much reliance on life jackets or rescues. That's one of the things we like about it. Everything you do, the consequences are direct and personal. You take precautions, you anticipate problems, and you deal with whatever happens. And you avoid doing anything stupid.

That's the reason it's hard to respect a fisherman like Alex. You can't put out a Mayday before you start heading for the rocks in the fog. He is creating his own dangers, and if he doesn't have enough sense to quit fishing, he probably deserves to die.

We're still heading in, and I don't see any rocks yet. Alex has slowed down to an idle and is looking for a break in the fog. By his calculations, we're almost there. I'm thinking about how cold the water is, and how much surge there is around the rocks even in a calm sea, which this is. I'm thinking about the breakers, and what my chances are of getting out of this alive. Then I see the first rock. I alert Alex, and he stops and just misses it. The fog starts to clear a little, and we can see more rocks, all around the boat. There are even rocks behind us that I don't know how we missed. They are reddish-brown, sandstone rocks. Now Alex and I both know exactly where we are: we're in Drake's Bay, in the breaker line, in the middle of hundreds of rocks, above and below the surface.

There are some places you just don't go in a boat, and this is one of them. Now that Alex has the reassurance of knowing where he is, it dawns on him that he was a lot better off not knowing, and being somewhere else. We're going to have to crawl out of here, and move very slowly, checking all around the boat before we move even a foot. I promise myself that if we get out of this, and back to any harbor, I'm getting off this boat.

It takes us over an hour of very careful maneuvering to back slowly out of this maze of rocks. It isn't even safe to turn around. I'm running around the boat and telling Alex where the rocks are as they appear through the fog. I could reach out and touch some of them. How we got in it without hitting one can only be attributed to St. Jude. I'm wondering where the hell was the fathometer when Alex was running us into this. It must have been bouncing up and down; why didn't he see it? Rocks or not, you don't even go into water this shallow unless you know exactly what's there.

He doesn't want to go in at Bodega, so I have to go all the way back to Noyo with him. It's better to end up at home, but if I had any alternative, I would take some other transportation. I sure miss Rudy.

I'm sorry to quit, because I probably won't find an opening on another boat until next season. Regardless, I would have to be suicidal to stay on this boat. I can accept the inherent dangers in fishing, because I want to escape the mundane, and find out what I'm made of. But I don't want to find out by getting cracked open on a rock. And especially not because of doing something stupid.

On the way home, I'm thinking about the close calls we've had. As a child, I used to think of myself as the reincarnation of my brother, Johnnie, and death didn't mean much to me. I'd just come back as someone else. I'm not convinced of that any more.

Whether or not I'm him, I don't plan to tell my parents much about the past few days, because it might cause flashbacks. I've seen a lot of signs over the years that they were never able to deal with losing Johnnie. (Having to fight calling me Johnnie the first three years of my life, for one thing.) Ironically, the reason they moved to Fort Bragg from Willows was for Johnnie's health.

When Johnnie was five, he got spinal meningitis and was in Children's Hospital in San Francisco for six months. My parents used to take the train from Willows every weekend to visit him. He was one of the few children to survive the disease, and when he was released from the hospital the doctors told my parents to move him to a cooler climate. They chose Fort Bragg, because my dad's family had spent summers there camping to get out of the Sacramento Valley heat. He knew the area and now had a sister living there.

People say everybody in Willows is related to everybody in Fort Bragg, but it only seems that way. Willows people are attracted to Fort Bragg, because when it's 110 degrees in Willows, the temperate coast is very appealing. Fort Bragg is due west, via State Highway 20, over the hills, past Clear Lake, and through the woods, about 250 miles.

My dad got a job in the mill and eventually became a saw filer. My mother worked part-time as a waitress, and probably never would have become a newspaper reporter except for the circumstances of Johnnie's death.

In 1946, when their 9-year-old son was killed, it was traditional here (and probably in other rural counties) to protect prominent citizens from recriminations for their minor transgressions, like drunk driving. Johnnie was killed by a prominent, older merchant who routinely had too much to drink, and continued to drive after his license was revoked. The young Robbins family were new arrivals (a status that in Fort Bragg takes about 30 years to shed), and didn't understand the workings of the community's sheltering of its own. They expected the man to be charged and punished. He had run over a child who was at least ten feet off the roadway, in a field, on his bicycle. Witnesses reported this, and a police officer took measurements at the scene.

As it happened, the one available doctor for a sobriety test was also Johnnie's regular physician, who had just received the emergency call and was on his way to the hospital. A sobriety test seemed unimportant to him at the time. He told the officer to get the man out of there, he had an emergency to respond to. So at the inquest, there was no evidence that the man was drunk. There were no measurements, because the officer had lost them.

If you have lost a nine-year-old son and endured a funeral with pall-bearers in Cub Scout uniforms, it's not going to make you feel better to see the old man who unintentionally caused the tragedy pay a price. On the other hand, it is intolerable to think that this could happen again at any time to someone else if this sort of behavior and indulgence isn't stopped. That thought also carries the salvation of action: something to do about this, when there is really nothing that will help in dealing with the grief.

My mother would normally have lacked the confidence to apply for a job as a reporter. She was an avid reader, but had to quit school at 16 to work. She had a severe hearing loss, and had worn a hearing aid since she was 20. This was a hereditary bone structure defect mainly in the women in her family. Some had been totally deaf, but she and her mother had partial hearing. Perhaps related to her hearing loss, her spelling was atrocious.

She had become friendly with a neighbor who was the local correspondent for the Press Democrat, the daily Santa Rosa newspaper delivered in Fort Bragg, who was moving from the area. Her friend encouraged her to apply, and convinced her that a really good reporter doesn't have to be able to spell. That's what copy editors are for.

She was a good reporter, and learned to be a great photographer. My dad set up a darkroom in the pantry and helped with her photo processing. He was never comfortable with the notoriety she had as a reporter, and the unwelcome recognition it gave him, but he was proud of her and as supportive as his reticent nature allowed.

For me it was a mixed blessing. As a kid I got to carry her heavy camera bag, so I never missed a hot news event. She knew everybody, so I could never get away with anything. Overall, it was probably a good thing for me that she had a lot of other things to occupy her time. She couldn't spend too much of it worrying about me, which she might otherwise have done. Luckily, Alex and I didn't make the news.

Alex finds another crewman, and keeps fishing. A couple of months after I quit, the St. Jude goes on the rocks. Alex survives that one too, but his crewman doesn't. Then I learn that Alex has now lost four boats in four seasons. I hope, for his sake and everybody else's, that he won't be able to get another boat. Alex has never done anything else except fish. He may think he's too old to learn to do something else. He should think about that. No matter what else he tried, he couldn't do much worse than he's doing now. In most other things, the consequences wouldn't be so grave, even if he failed miserably.

Out of curiosity, I check the encyclopedia, and find out that somebody named Jude was the author of the New Testament epistle filled with warnings against deceivers. That's when I find out that St. Jude was considered the patron saint of desperate causes. If that boat had a different name, and if I had to try now to find an apt and symbolic name for the vessel that carried Alex Johnson, I would call it the St. Jude.

CHAPTER 6

LONGLINING, WESTERN STYLE

Believe me! The secret of reaping the greatest fruitfulness and the greatest enjoyment from life is to live dangerously.
Friedrich Nietzsche

1966-72

Rudy welcomes me back to the Driftwood, and I fish with him off and on for the next couple of years. I have to work a few other jobs to make enough money, because Rudy only fishes when he feels like it. Even at the height of salmon season, money doesn't motivate him unless he's broke or close to it. He likes to keep his life simple, and he doesn't need much to live on. Now I can appreciate the simplicity of the Driftwood, too. I've had the bigger boat experience, and I'm not so impatient.

I've taken Rudy home for dinner a few times, and he has become pretty good friends with my parents. He takes them a salmon or a ling cod and drops by for a visit whether I'm around or not. When he talks to my parents, I hear his opinions about things he and I usually don't talk about. I'm amazed at how naive his views are about almost everything but fishing.

My mother is a reporter for the Santa Rosa Press Democrat, the only daily paper delivered in Fort Bragg, so she and my dad are well informed and interested in politics. When they discuss politics with Rudy, his opinions reflect almost complete trust that whoever is making the decisions must surely know what they are doing. He doesn't have any interest in taking part in politics, mainly because he doesn't feel qualified in that area. But what astonishes me is that he seems to believe that the people who do are all as competent at it as he is at fishing, and he can comfortably leave it to them. He wouldn't presume to question it, because they are in their area of expertise that he knows nothing about.

His self-effacing attitude goes beyond politics, into almost every area besides boats and fishing and the ocean. He doesn't have opinions about the things he lacks expertise in, and leaves them to the experts. He knows something about wood carving, so he will give you opinions about that. But he doesn't feel he's entitled to an opinion unless he has a lot of experience or knowledge in the area being discussed. This is a new concept to me.

Growing up in the household I did, I've never met anyone who is so reticent about trusting his own judgment. It shocks me. Rudy has exceptional common sense, and that alone gives him more right to an opinion than a lot of people I know who freely express themselves on every subject. I guess that's part of how Rudy keeps his life so simple--staying completely out of things he knows nothing about.

Unlike Rudy's, my life is starting to get complicated. My biggest expense is car insurance, but my girlfriend, Vi, and I are planning to get married. In the spring of 1969, Vi sets the wedding date for October. Since I don't have a steady job on a boat that fishes year around--or even all of the salmon season--I decide I'd better get a job on land. I don't have any preferences, so I decide to take the first thing that comes along.

Heritage House, 1969
A Break from Fishing

Being a dishwasher--even at an exclusive, world class hideaway inn--isn't my idea of excitement and adventure, but that's what comes along first. The only danger involved is driving there. Heritage House is on scenic State Highway 1, a narrow road along rocky cliffs that compares with the upper corniche on the French Riviera. It's about 25 miles from Fort Bragg, and I often have to drive to work in soupy fog.

The inn and surrounding cottages are in an idyllic setting above a spectacular ocean cove. The bar has what may be the world's most beautiful ocean view. You could argue about that, but see it first. The windows overlook the cove, and you can see the waves breaking high up the rocks and smell the spray. It's not one of those distant, panoramic views; you're right on the edge. The inn is a historic home, but the cottages were built later, though they look like they belong and were always there. The perfection of the setting is no accident; Richard Dennen, who had the cottages built, was a set designer in Hollywood before he acquired the family place. It's such a classic dream location for clandestine romance, they filmed a movie about one there called "Same Time Next Year."

Meeting Dennen is worth the humility of a dishwasher's job, because he's another individual like Rudy and Tony who does what he does better than anyone else could ever do it. You always learn valuable things from people like that, even if they are not always easy to work for.

I pick up some culture here, because at Heritage House, even the dishwasher has to have class. I dress better here to wash dishes than I would have for the high school prom. One of my perks is getting to wash Mr. Dennen's Ferrari, which means I have to drive it a few yards. I'm driving an early bathtub Porsche now, so I'm getting closer to my dream car, but it's still a ways off for me. It's really a treat to have a chance to actually touch a Ferrari.

Heritage House is low key. Few local residents even know it's open to the public for dinner. Most of the patrons are guests of the inn. The regular clientele is in a tax bracket that, in this area, is almost nonexistent. Only a few people would qualify, like maybe Union Lumber Company's top management, who are owners. Some of the regulars are Hollywood stars, and wealthy San Francisco socialites. I might go to work and see Perry Mason. I'm cool, though, and treat celebrities like ordinary human beings while catering to them as though they were gods, as the Dennens require.

It's a revelation to me to be around celebrities for the first time. I guess I expected maturity because of their high social status. My illusions are shattered when I hear one of them complain that someone else's salad has more croutons than theirs. The waiter rushes to the kitchen and gets a small bowl of croutons just for them, and everything is fine. There are never any complaints of substance, because the food and service are always perfect; the Dennens make sure of that.

I don't stay a dishwasher long. One day the back-up chef fails to show up for work, and Mr. Dennen asks me to sharpen a knife so he can personally carve the prime rib. Thanks to Tony, I know how to sharpen a knife. The prime rib cuts like butter. Mr. Dennen has probably never handled a knife that sharp. Suddenly I'm promoted to back-up chef, without even a day at cooking school.

Six months later I'm a creditable chef. Mr. Dennen buys the Mendocino Hotel, and I find myself in charge of the kitchen as temporary chef, until he can arrange for a notable one. I'm not in danger of a permanent career change, but I enjoy it for a while. I've learned a valuable skill, but in my heart I'm still a fisherman. As a chef, not only do I know what I'll be doing tomorrow; I have to know what I'll be doing for the whole week, and have a plan for the entire month. It's no job for a fisherman.

Meanwhile, I take some night classes in welding, and one of my dad's friends offers me a job as a millwright. I have some resistance to taking it, because that's where everybody has always thought I belonged, and I don't want to prove them right. I do it anyway, because it pays more than double my chef's job, and it's more interesting. A millwright is a trouble-shooter who gets called to fix anything that breaks, so there's always a challenge. So I've been doing that for a couple of years.

Then another opportunity comes along. The owner of the steam laundry wants me to quit the mill and go to work for him. He thinks a "jack of all trades" is exactly what the laundry needs, and he offers me more money than

I'm earning at the mill. It sounds boring to me, but I like Homer, the owner, and the money is good, so I decide to try it.

I'm pretty successful at keeping all the old equipment running, and I get along with all the other employees, mainly women in their 40s and 50s who have known me all my life. He seems to think I'm doing okay, except that we have a run-in now and then. He confronts me one day because I'm including my lunch hour on my time card. I tell him it says in the Labor Code that on your lunch hour you have to be "relieved of all duties." I have to watch the boiler, don't I? He agrees that I do.

Before long we understand each other, and one day he tells me he's going to retire, and approaches me about buying the business from him. I think he's joking--I don't have five bucks--but he convinces me he isn't.

He says we'll go together and talk to the banker tomorrow. I tell him I don't have a suit, or even dress clothes. I never go anywhere that I can't wear jeans. He says you never dress up for a banker. You need to be comfortable when you talk to a banker, and if anybody is uncomfortable, it should be him.

I go home and discuss it with Vi and we get pretty enthusiastic. She works in an office and can help me with the business part. I go over to discuss it with my parents. My mother is encouraging, but my dad is very conservative about taking on any financial obligation. They lived in a rented house for 16 years, until he was sure he could make house payments. I know he got that way from going through the Great Depression, but I'm still impatient with his extreme caution. I'm thinking, "What have I got to lose? I have nothing, and if somebody wants to give me a chance to parlay it into something, why not try it." So I said something sarcastic, like, "Well, Dad, maybe I'll wait 20 years and see if I get another chance."

Our conversations often ended like this, and we both felt bad about it. On some subjects there's just too much of a chasm to bridge between us. He takes debt so seriously. He'd be like Socrates: after drinking the hemlock cup, he'd say, "I owe a cock to Aesculapius. Will you remember to pay the debt." That's not what I'd be thinking about.

Homer and I go see the banker. He and I know each other, even though we travel in different circles--his being the Chamber of Commerce and Rotary Club. He's not much older than I am, and we both drive Porsches. I get the money for the deal Homer has worked out, and I'm a business man. I'm under 30 and I own the laundry.

Vi's father has recently retired as Postmaster, so he is ready to figure out what the profit margin has to be and put me on the budget we need to be on, and oversee the bookkeeping. Things go pretty well for a couple of years, at least financially. We won't talk about how much I like mediating disputes between women who could be my mother or grandmother, and dealing with motel owners who try to find ways to get out of paying some of their laundry bills. Or having so many other people involved in every decision I make.

One weekend Vi and I decide we're ready to get our Ferrari. We drive to Mozart Motors in Marin County to look at previously owned sports cars. They have a red Ferrari that looks a lot like the one Dennen had, a little older, but well cared for. We look at the sticker price, and it's under what we agreed we could pay. Vi expects me to buy it, but she leaves it up to me. It's my dream, and she just goes along with it. She would drive a beige Ford Falcon or a Plymouth and be happy, because she looks at a car as strictly utilitarian.

I'm thinking about the Ferrari having to run around town in second gear, and never getting to open up like it's made to do. I'm imagining parking it by the laundry, and worrying about getting a dent in it. I'm picturing myself as a hot shot Ferrari owner, an arrogant kid that would invite resentment. I can live with that, because I really want that Ferrari. Or do I?

Now I'm looking at a green Lotus Elan with an identical price tag. I open the door and sit down in the Lotus. If my feet were any bigger than size 8, they wouldn't fit the floor pedals of this car. I haven't run across many advantages in this life to being small. Here's one.

I've seen one or two Ferraris in Fort Bragg from time to time. I have never seen a Lotus in Fort Bragg. Most people in Fort Bragg don't know what a Lotus Elan is. I decide to test drive it. It's made of fiberglass and wouldn't survive any impact. No use even worrying about scratches. For a few minutes I savor the idea that I can have the Ferrari if I want it. We test drive it, and I tell Vi I want the Lotus.

We trade in the Porsche and drive home in the Lotus. We still have an El Camino pickup for practical driving. We leave Mozart Motors without the Ferrari, and with no regrets.

Vi and I have a lot of fun driving the Lotus up and down the coast, and our friends are impressed. My dad's only comment when he sees it is, "It won't haul much wood." That's the typical Mendocino Coast measure of the worth of a vehicle. Dad never accepted a ride in it, and he persisted in calling it "the green locust" all the time we had it. That didn't bother me. We laughed about it. When we finally sold it, the Ferrari was out of my system. I finally realized I get tired of cars and just like a change more often than other people. I found out it runs in the Rice family. My uncles bought a new car every year, and the surprise was, so did their father. My mother said they were dirt poor as kids, but they always had a new car.

We've been prospering, but then the laundry business begins to sour in Fort Bragg. The tourist trade is growing, there are more motels, so now laundries from Ukiah and Santa Rosa want to cut in on the business. They have capital and I don't, and they offer to buy all the linens for my customers. I start losing them, one by one, and I finally have to either make a big investment--which I don't have--or close the laundry to stop losing money. I feel sad for the employees who depend on the laundry and have been so loyal. But I feel ecstatic for me. I've been hating the laundry business for some time. We manage to sell the equipment and pay off the bank, but we don't come out of it with anything except some wisdom we didn't have before. Some would say my dad was right, but I'd do it again. I wouldn't have the experience--or the Ferrari dream realized--if I hadn't done it.

Vi knows I miss fishing. She would prefer having me work on land, but she's pretty understanding about how I feel about it. She watched me race dirt bikes, and do all the other foolhardy things I used to do, so she knows I'm never going to be happy as chef or millwright or laundryman. So she agrees when I decide to go back to fishing.

Fishing is the one job that ideally suits my nature. I'm not pushing myself beyond my threshold of fear to impress my peers, like I did as a kid climbing trees or riding bicycles or motorcycles. I'm not taking foolish, unnecessary risks. Fishing legitimizes my need for excitement. It's just a requirement of the job to accept the risks inherent in going to sea. If you're unable to do that with some nobility, you don't belong to the brotherhood. You could give it up out of dread, and still be respected. But if you can't face the fear with strength, nobody wants you out there. Especially not on their boat. I can, and I intend to prove it, if only to myself.

Winter, 1973
Back to Fishing

I have some experience now, so I can be a little more selective about boats and skippers. Ollie Jensen needs a crewman. His reputation passes my seamanship test, and his boat, the Helga II, is sound and seaworthy. Ollie fishes both salmon and albacore, and in the winter he uses longline gear to fish close to shore for bottom fish. I'm aware of the dangers of fishing close to the rocks, and I want to learn it with somebody cautious and experienced. Ollie is probably a good person to learn it from.

I'm not picking skippers for affability now, or Ollie wouldn't be my choice. Ollie looks at everything and everybody with a glare. I've never seen him when he wasn't glaring. Even when he's drunk, he's glaring; it's just a softer glare.

The condition is that I help him repair the longline gear, and help him put the new engine in his boat. I thought that was probably the reason he didn't have other people applying for the job. As a crewman, you don't get paid for anything but fish; you're expected to help with boat repairs. But if you need a job right away, you probably can't wait around for major repairs. I can wait. We have a little money saved, and Vi says her job at the telephone company can pay the bills for a while. I'll get some work in the winter, and later the chance to do some serious albacore fishing. It takes a bigger boat to fish albacore, because you have to go out farther and stay out longer than for salmon, so I haven't done any albacore fishing yet. I didn't stay on the St. Jude long enough. (Lucky for me. As it turned out, the St. Jude didn't make it to albacore season.)

Ollie is dour and never says much, not even "good morning", so I quit trying to make conversation with him. I have a lot of experience making my junker cars run, so I'm a good mechanic and he seems satisfied. We get the engine installed and the gear ready, and I soon have the most exciting fishing lessons of my life.

If you're familiar with longlining for swordfish in the north Atlantic, you're thinking of miles of line and hooks a long distance apart. This is the same general idea, but we use tub gear and the main line is a quarter-mile long, with about 150 hooks only 18 inches apart on 10-inch leaders. We set the lines in close near the rocks, less than a quarter mile from shore. The main line is quarter-inch nylon rope, and the leaders are short and heavy, nylon cord about 150 pound test. We're fishing for snapper, rock cod, and ling cod.

There are three tubs to a set, tied together, all on one long line, with anchors at both ends, and a flag and buoy on one end so we can find them. Every fishermen has his own color flags; some of their wives make them. We set the gear by 10 or 11 in the morning, and then go back to the beginning and pick it up.

We have about 50 tubs on the boat, on special racks built to hold them so they don't get spilled or tangled. The racks take the whole length of the after deck. Some are even stored on the bow to get them out of the way.

In the morning from the time we leave the harbor we're baiting the hooks. We use cut bait, fish cut in chunks about an inch square, usually herring or smelt. When we start, the hooks are carefully positioned, stuck in the cork rim at the top of the tub. The leaders are called gangions, pronounced like "canyons". The gangions are long enough to allow the main line to be coiled in the bottom of the tub. The tub looks like a very neat pincushion. You take the first hook out, put the bait on, and hang the hook over the edge of the tub the same place it came from, but no longer stuck in the edge. You leave a half-inch gap between each baited hook, and it's critical that they stay in order.

When you get to the fishing grounds you set the gear, usually in 5 to 25 fathoms over a rock pile. There are loops in both ends of the main line. You take the top loop out of the tub and tie it to an anchor line with 50 fathoms of 1/4 inch rope, and tie the end loop of that tub (which should have been laid in there so it's accessible without tangling up all that line) to the top loop of the next tub, and then a third one, until you have a set of three tubs, and tie the third tub to a second anchor line, which has a buoy and a flag. You tie everything together and get it ready to go in the water in preparation for setting out the gear.

The flags are on bamboo poles 10 feet high. They are just rags, but all the same color so whenever you see that color you know whose gear it is. Some make the flags look more like flags than rags, but not many. If they're too prissy the fisherman takes some ribbing, not only from the other fishermen, but from his own crew. If he continues to use perfect little flags, year after year, you know he has a good sense of humor and a solid marriage.

The spooky part is getting all that gear in the water without a tangle. If one of the hooks catches you, it can pull you right over the stern of the boat; you'd be in the water before you knew what happened. Or it could go clear through your hand. They are 4-ought hooks.

I can't explain hook sizes. They go from small to large 1, 2, 3, 4, and then start with 1/0, 2/0, 3/0, 4/0. Norwegians or Swedes are probably responsible for it.

There must be some logic to it. To me, it's about as clear as the Muppets Swedish chef. But the hooks we use are about 1 to 1-1/2 inches across the gap between the hook point and the shank. The length of the shank varies from about 4 to 6 inches, and we pick the length to use depending on the size of the bait we have. If we can get small enough herring we use them instead of cut bait.

The skipper has already scouted the area when you're ready to set. He has decided where, and will get over that spot and he'll say, "Now," and you throw the first anchor over. Setting is done about half-throttle (4 knots) so the gear doesn't end up piled on top of itself. It's even more critical if you're in deep water to string it out well. The hooks are close together, and that line has to go out there fairly snug.

Before you set, you put a knife in your teeth. It seems dramatic, but it's no joke; it's the only place you can put it where you can get it fast enough to cut a gangion if a hook sticks in your hand. If you get a hook stuck in your hand, the line is tight in a split second. It's all you can do to hold it back--if you can. But when a nylon line is that taut, all it takes is a tap with a sharp knife to cut it. You've got to be ready.

The first month, I got stuck in the side of my index finger twice, and cut the line both times without missing a beat. You just lose a hook; you've got 150 of them per tub. It's like a Bruce Willis action movie; you react to the pain later when the excitement is over.

Once that anchor is thrown overboard, things start happening fast. You pick up the first tub and rotate it, turned at an angle toward the water to keep the hooks coming out on the bottom. They whip out fast. When you get to the last 4 or 5 hooks in that tub, you set that tub down by your feet and quickly grab the second tub so you can get it in position. You do the same with the third.

At the end of the third tub, you grab the anchor. They are about 15 pounds, scrap iron in all shapes and sizes. You don't use anything you're afraid to lose. We use window weights, anything.

The boat is still going 4 or 5 knots. You hold the anchor as long as you comfortably can hold it back, which is about two seconds, and then let go. You grab ahold of the boom or anything to brace yourself. Then 50 feet of line and a buoy goes out, and you throw the buoy over. Once you get the last tub out, you're home free; the anchor is pretty simple stuff.

This is all done standing up on deck. The gaff hatch is sealed off for longlining. When you're not landing fish you don't need to reach the water. It's easier to work at the same height all the time when you're doing this precision stuff so fast, and you need room.

This is how it goes when everything is like it's supposed to be. What you always have to realize is that if anything isn't exactly in position precisely where it belongs, you're in a lot of trouble. If one hook gets out of place, or the tub is coiled wrong, one comes out somewhere and takes a whole tangle with it. When this happens, you let go of the whole tub; in fact, you throw it.

You get rid of it, and get out of the way, because you don't know where the next hook is coming from. In the beginning I always felt like I'd really accomplished something if I lived until noon.

Picking up, everything is a lot slower. The lines come up over the side over a roller. The line makes one loop around a capstan, and then it's coiled. It's motor driven. One man stands between the winch and the rail of the boat and takes fish off the hook using a gaff hook. He might have to gaff a big fish, but most of them just come over the side. You grab the line, take the gaff and put it in the bend of the hook, keep the line tight and pull the gaff up, give one snap and the fish will fall off. Someone skilled with a gaff can unhook the fish very fast. Some hardly jerk, they just drop the fish, then lift up and turn their wrist a little. You use a deft motion keeping the line tight, or the hook will turn over.

The deck hand, called the puller, stands behind the capstan, recoiling the line in the tub. The hard thing to do is keep constant tension on the line when it comes in. Tension is the only thing that keeps it from slipping right around the capstan and going to the bottom. It doesn't take a lot of tension, just steady tension. Using both hands, you loop the line in the tub, set the hook, loop in the tub, set the hook, keeping tension on the line. The line is made to coil that way, and can be trained. It's called "hard lay nylon". It's not pliable, but very stiff like a lariat, and you make each coil identical. Then the gear will go out just like it went in.

You untie the flag poles and store them in rat lines (cable or rope ladders with wooden steps). On the way in, you put everything back where it belongs. This is a job where neatness counts.

Other fishermen get to know where you're setting your gear, and don't set theirs where you're accustomed to fishing, even if you're not there that day. You don't screw anybody else up, especially not the crab fishermen. The crab season is so short, it's harder to make a living. There are more places within a given area where a longline fisherman can set, and maybe only two or three places where a crab fisherman can set crab pots. They have to have a sandy bottom near the rocks. You go out of your way to try to help them, and you try not to offend anybody else by infringing on their territory.

You try to avoid anyone else's gear, but it will drift in bad weather. Once in a while you might get yours tangled up with a crab pot, but a crab fisherman will not set in the same place you are longlining. He would just go someplace else if you were already there.

Longlining isn't as profitable as salmon or albacore because the fish aren't worth as much. The fish are in better shape than they are from trawlers, and the fish are sold as fresh market fish. Bottom fish just don't bring the price of salmon or albacore, but it's worth doing if you want to fish in the winter. It's dangerous fishing close to the rocks in rough winter seas. We can only go out about a third of the time; the rest of the time it's too risky because of the weather.

Once in a while we get tidal surges in the harbor, and whenever we got advance word of one coming the skippers would take their boats out and ride the wave out at sea, rather than leave their boats tied to the docks where they might get damaged. We didn't always know what caused them, maybe an earthquake somewhere, or maybe the moon was just doing figure eights. Usually they were hardly perceptible at sea, but there would be a big wave into the harbor. It was a deep, narrow harbor, and usually there wasn't much damage to the boats. It was just prudent to take the boats out until it was over.

When the big earthquake hit Alaska on March 27, 1964, a resulting tsunami (we called them "tidal waves" then) did a lot of damage to Kodiak Island and Anchorage, and was heading down the California coast. Fishing boats that were out off Alaska at the time had to go down to Seattle, where there wasn't much damage, to unload their catch. We had plenty of warning of the coming wave, because the following morning we got reports that it had wiped out more than fifty blocks in the main part of Crescent City. Everybody took their boats out of Noyo Harbor. It was like a big boat parade. I think it's the first time I ever saw every boat at Noyo out at the same time.

I was still working for Tony then, and he sent us home. I was watching from up by Noyo bridge. The fishermen all said that when the wave came, it was hard to identify. It was just a few feet higher than the other waves. After it went by, they just waited a while and took the boats back into the harbor.

It's a good thing it was anti-climactic, because there were people gathered near the beach and all over Noyo flat to see the tidal wave, even after they heard what it did to Crescent City. There was even more damage to boats at Crescent City than there should have been, because a lot of them failed to heed the warning and take their boats out. After their experience, at least the fishermen here took the warning seriously.

The harbor at Crescent City is a lot different from Noyo. It's shallow for a long way offshore, and a big wave makes a much greater impression there. At Noyo it's deep for a long way into shore, and the channel is deep and narrow. It made a pretty big surge into the channel, but not high enough to do any major damage to the docks or buildings. The boats would have been banged around if they had been there when it hit.

I never get any feedback from the skipper. Fishing with him is grim, but I'm learning a lot and I don't mind. I know how I'm doing. I respect his seamanship, and I'm usually cheerful in spite of him. I get paid regularly. We're not here for companionship, but it is wearing sometimes being around him. I've never once seen him smile, even when we're having a good salmon season, and everybody else is smiling a lot around Noyo.

One of the things I like best about fishing is that it's so simple. You don't have to wonder how you're doing, like with some other jobs. You pull in a couple of salmon, and that pays for the ice and fuel. The next one pays for the groceries. A couple more hit the deck, and you're in the money. You can tell what they're worth by the size. You can mentally total them up at the end of a trip and figure out roughly what 15 percent will come to, and that's going to be your paycheck.

I'm looking forward to albacore fishing, and the season is coming up. We'll be staying out longer and going farther, and it will broaden my horizons. I'm still enthusiastic, but now I think I know why Ollie didn't have a lot of choices when he needed a crewman. If I had known him better at the time, I still would have taken the job. The Helga II is the most seaworthy boat I've ever been on, and Ollie is a very competent skipper. It's amazing what experience will do to adjust your priorities.

CHAPTER 7

STORM

Trips like this are rare. If they were common, most of us would probably find another line of work. This was not the "storm of the century", but it was at least the storm of the decade in albacore season when the boats were out. We lost four boats from our fleet. Every fisherman has his worst storm: this was mine.

Fall 1974

Ollie hates fishing for all the same reasons I thrive on it. The uncertainty of it is just frustrating for him. Every day something comes up that makes it not quite like it should be. That's what makes it interesting. The sea is never the same as it was the day before, and there are differences from one place to another. You never know what's going to happen. It's like having a cyclone one day and an earthquake the next, and trying to do your job as usual. Ollie doesn't like that, and it irritates him that I do.

We can go for ten days without speaking--which isn't easy on a 47-foot boat when you seldom get more than 20 feet apart. We aren't having a very good season. He won't go out if it even looks like it might blow. We're always in the wrong place, or a day behind the fleet. I don't respect his fishing decisions, but if he asks me if we should run north or south, I won't say. Whenever I do, he argues with me and does something else. So I just say, "You're the skipper," and he quits asking.

Putting up with me is just one more sign of how passive he is, hating everything, and doing it anyway. He might not have liked anyone else any better. When he gets cuts he rinses his hands in Clorox every night. He does it to show how manly he is. When we're in port with other fishermen, I call him "Captain Flint," but not to his face. They all know who I'm talking about. They say, "How can you fish with that sour s.o.b.?" I respect his seamanship and his boat.

The Helga II is an ex-Alaskan halibut schooner, 47 feet long and narrow for her size. She's a very deep boat and draws 8 feet of water. She's quite seaworthy because of her depth, but because of that she's a very uncomfortable boat even in a moderate sea. But the ride doesn't get much more uncomfortable as the sea gets worse. She was not built for a comfortable motion; rather, to survive any Pacific storm. Fishermen call these boats "holy rollers", but it's not disrespectful, just descriptive. Ollie made the money to buy the Helga II fishing halibut in Alaska in an open 20-foot boat, with hand lines. That could be why he thinks life is miserable.

Trolling for albacore is fun. It's all about speed. Albacore travel fast, and you can see a school of them from a distance when they're feeding on squid near the surface. The water looks choppy. We troll for them with jigs just below the surface. The jig is just a lure that looks like a chrome lug nut on a car wheel, with a rubber skirt to look like squid tentacles, and a double hook with no barb. We run two or three poles off the stern, with six or eight lines. The wider the boat, the more lines you can run. But you can only have so many, with jigs skipping along almost at the surface, without getting them tangled. We trail them at 6 or 7 knots, and they're just under the surface, not deep and weighted like salmon lines. What the albacore sees is a small school of squid behind the boat.

We can't use mechanized gear like we do for salmon. Trolling for albacore is fast to keep up with the fast fish, and you have to land them fast too. Salmon have delicate mouths, and you would lose them on a barbless hook, but albacore are tough fish, and when they bite the pressure of stretching their fins out secures them on the hook if you get them up fast. The barbless hook means you can get them out of the fish quickly. They fall right off when you get them on board, and you throw the jig right back in the water. Each albacore is on its own line, and you pull them up hand over hand as fast as you can, as hard as you can, skipping them along the surface. If they get their fins spread, you're in trouble. They will sound (dive) like a whale, if they get a chance.

Sometimes you've only got fifteen or twenty minutes with a school, unless it's a really big one, because they are so fast. They get bored with your silly little school of squid and take off, or get spooked. In a big school, you can be landing albacore all day. They school by size, so whatever you're into, they will all be the same size. Between 10 and 15 pounds is about average. We call the 7 to 9 pound ones peanuts. The bigger ones are usually about 30 pounds.

Speed is really important, because when you're in a big school you can land 50 fish an hour per person, and sometimes even more. One day we were really into them from daylight to dark, and caught 1100 fish. I don't know how only two of us did it. You're pulling the lines hand over hand as fast as you can, all day, and your hands are bleeding. You don't care if you drop dead. You're seeing nothing but dollar signs, making up for all the days when you didn't catch enough to pay for your fuel and ice. I'd run in and grab a salami, take a bite, and pull in some more albacore.

We use 3-inch wide sections of bicycle inner tube to protect our hands from cuts. It keeps your palm protected and your fingers free. We land albacore like pulling a bucket up over a well, hand over hand. The rubber and the monofilament line don't slide on each other. You never wrap a line around your hand, no matter what kind of fishing you're doing. Something big like a shark could grab the line, and it would take your hand off. For albacore we're using 120 pound test, the same diameter line that's most often in a string trimmer for cutting weeds.

The first albacore I caught was such a beautiful creature, I had an impulse to throw it back and let it live-- just momentarily. They're sleek and beautiful. They look like a bullet, pointed on both ends, with a tail. Their fins are half the length of their body, narrow, about two inches wide, like wings. If they get under the surface and get those wings spread when you're trying to land them, it's like slamming on disc brakes, so you have to be fast. They have a ridge on top that is dark blue, almost black, that fades to a lighter blue, and the rest is a bright silver. They look a little like a flying fish. Their color is brighter when they first come out of the water, and they're luminous. They're so striking, you wouldn't want to kill them if you didn't need to. I had a feeling of appreciation for them, like the native plainsmen did for the buffalo. I think a lot of fishermen do.

I soon learn that Ollie will never spend money on the boat when he needs to, and we're often stuck in some harbor with a problem he should have fixed at home. We're often a day behind the fleet. One day can cost you $10,000 if you're a day behind the fleet following albacore. There might be 20 to 300 boats in a pack, and albacore travel fast. You can go for days before they stop catching fish and stop running, so you can catch up. There's a much better chance of finding fish if you're with them, and a good skipper can stay with a school of albacore for a long time. It's costly to miss all the action, and Ollie is even harder to be around when he knows its his fault.

We don't normally have to think about measuring water temperature trying to find the fish, because we're usually running to where other people are catching albacore, or trolling in the water over 60 degrees where they're already known to be. It's only necessary to worry about temperature when you're looking for fish that aren't around yet.

Every year the fishermen's association puts aside some of the dues money and pays for fuel for a few boats to scout the albacore before the salmon season is over. The scout boats leave salmon season early, usually mid-July, to find the albacore. They start looking in the Japanese current below Monterey, where albacore first begin to show up. If they radio the fleet and dealers that they're catching albacore off Bodega Head, 40 fish a day, it's not worth leaving salmon for. But for 70 to 100, it probably is.

On this trip the weather is pretty fair as we go out. There are a few whitecaps, but by the time we get out as far as you have to go for albacore it can be altogether different, and it can change completely in a day. There's no reason not to go out. There is certainly no indication of what is to come.

We go out about 220 miles, about a day and a half running time, and we're fishing albacore off Cape Blanco on the Oregon coast. We have lots of fuel and groceries-- enough for about ten days. We have water to last a month, and enough food for a few extra meals. We are with a fairly large fleet, about 30 boats, but we're not fishing together. It's a loose knit fleet covering about 50 square miles, none of which are usually within sight, but we are within radio range of each other.

Every morning when you're fishing you notice the wind. When the wind starts blowing in the morning, it never dies down--it just builds. The earlier it comes up, the more likely it is to be blowing hard by noon. It's up early again today, and Ollie is swearing. When it's blowing, you get tossed around and it's difficult to fish. I'm thinking it would be nice if it would stop so it would be easier to fish, but it's kind of exciting. It has been blowing "small craft" every day, and on the fourth day it goes to gale warnings. That's no big deal.

Weather moves from west to east, so whatever they're reporting we've already had. We're also right at the southernmost point of the range they're reporting weather for that covers the Oregon and Washington coast north of us. The reports say, "Gale warnings from Tatoosh to Cape Blanco for west to southwest winds, "etc.

Cape Blanco Lighthouse is a weather station at the southern limit of the winter storms that strike the northern Pacific Northwest coast on a very well-defined track. The storm centers regularly sweep into shore between the Strait of Juan de Fuca and Grays Harbor in Washington. Off Blanco, we're probably going to be in the outer limits of whatever is going on north of us, just on the edge of it. If we were fishing salmon we would have gone in, primarily because salmon don't bite in this kind of weather; but albacore do.

We are committed, being this far out. It's a day and a half going in and your ice melts, you use up your supplies, and you have another day and a half getting back out. But it's not much fun fishing in a gale. If we were low on supplies we would take advantage of this kind of weather to go in and ice up and fuel up.

Old Flint is getting edgy. I can tell by the way he's throwing things around on deck that my cheerful humming is getting on his nerves. I'm bustling around getting the gear ready. He threw a rope down, and then later he tripped on it and swore. You never throw anything around on a fishing boat, for just that reason. You don't even throw matches on deck, because if you do they will end up in your bilge pumps and the pumps won't work when you need them. He has been fishing for 20 or 30 years; he's obviously irritated or he wouldn't have done it. I don't say anything, but he knows what I'm thinking.

By morning the swells are getting bigger and the wind is still picking up. It's over 30 knots, and it's impossible to fish. We're keeping in loose touch with the other boats on the radio and paying a lot more attention to the weather reports. The weather reports are not very accurate. They take wind speeds on points of land, and we are far removed from whatever is going on there. There's so much difference in the weather 200 miles offshore, you could be on another shoreline. By afternoon, they are reporting moderate gale winds, 40 to 45 knots, but we're getting a lot worse than that. It's getting risky to walk around on deck, and even hard to maintain your footing in the cabin.

Charlie Holt's boat is the biggest in the fleet, an 80-footer, and it has a weather machine on it with a windspeed meter. Charlie gives us reports about every hour, and I'm starting to wish he wouldn't. They are getting scarier. The sky is darkening, and black clouds are drifting toward us. Some of the boats are heading in, and the rest are talking about it. We are thinking about it.

The normal fisherman's outlook on heavy weather is not the same as most sailors or yachtsmen have who go to sea for recreation. A yachtsman wants to know exactly how high the waves are, and how fast the wind is blowing. He wants to know just what he and his boat have endured, so he can compare notes with other sailors or with things he has read. A fisherman, on the other hand, would rather not know. If it's possible to fish, he wants to keep fishing until he can't do it any more. He doesn't want to stop fishing because the radio tells him it's a gale. When it's so rough he can't fish any longer, he wants to know only as much as he needs to decide if he can wait it out, or if he has to get in behind some shelter or go back into port. Generally, a fisherman is very focused on why he is out there. He gets all the adventure he needs day to day; he doesn't savor it like he might if he only did it on weekends--or like I do.

Soon we're getting enough excitement even for me. I've never seen 40-foot swells before, and they are awesome. Our poles are 60 feet high, and the boat nearest in front of us completely disappears between swells. His poles are 60 feet high, too. There isn't anything in your life that prepares you for 40-foot swells--not even 30-foot swells. I can't believe I'm really seeing the keel of the other boat. We stay pretty far apart, and even farther apart at night when we drift. But tonight you wouldn't call it drifting.

Tonight before dark, Ollie and I both start nailing things down. We don't discuss it; we just start doing it. Before we shut down, all the hatches are nailed down: not just lashed down, nailed down; because it's obvious it is still building and it's going to get worse. We've never done that before.

We're exhausted by the time we finish, just from fighting the motion. The boat was pitching so much it was like trying to nail moving objects while swinging from monkey bars. We had to do everything with one hand and hold on with the other.

The Helga II has 18-inch deck rails, shin height, the perfect height for tripping you and throwing you in the briny. Most of the newer boats have waist-high rails. The lower ones are more convenient for fishing, but you have to be more careful. We always put lifelines up at waist level as soon as we start fishing. You can lean under them to gaff a fish or reach over the side for something. But when the weather is heavy, you never let go of the boom. There is a hand line on the boom to hold onto going from the house to the stern. There is never any reason to go forward unless you're anchoring, and then everything is perfectly safe. We couldn't anchor out here, needless to say, because that much rope or cable would have filled our entire ice hold. While we were nailing things down, we were grasping the handhold, feeling something like rodeo stars. It was quite a ride. There was enough water coming over to keep the decks awash and slippery even then.

Before we go to bed we hear a woman on the radio telling us the winds are a moderate 25 to 30 knots, when our steady sail is about to tear off the mast. Then Charlie reports that the windspeed is 60 knots, and that he is giving serious consideration to wasting his ice and fuel for this trip. A few more decide to head in. We tell them we think we'll see what it's like in the morning.

When we go to bed we have the steady sail up. The steady sail is a fixed sail on the boom, not designed to propel the boat, just to hold it steady. The boom doesn't move on most fishing boats; it's a brace for the mast and part of the standing rigging (unlike on a sailboat, where it's part of the running rigging). All the sail does is keep the boat heeled over slightly. The pressure on the sail keeps the boat steady. Without the sail, we would whip back and forth with every swell and bob too much. With the sail up, there's a snap to the roll of the boat on the leeward side as it rolls away from the wind, but it slows down the motion of the boat coming back up. The boat is laying in the trough, and I'm sleeping with my leg wedged against the deck beam to keep from being thrown out of my bunk.

During the night it goes to full storm warnings, and I picture a square red flag with a black center on the Coast Guard Station. They put up one flag, a red pennant, for small craft warnings, which is anything dangerous to small craft, including gusts, up to 33 knot winds. Two red pennants means gale warnings, 34 to 47 knots. A square red flag with a black center means storm, which is 48 knots and above--no matter how much above. You never see two storm flags on the Coast Guard Station on this coast, because that is reserved for winds in connection with a tropical cyclone, of which a hurricane is one type. We don't have those here, so whatever we get is just called a storm--even if it's stronger than hurricane-force winds. We have to take our storm warnings seriously.

Winds above 64 knots are characteristic of hurricanes, and those conditions mean imminent danger, death; no boats under 40 feet long allowed out of the harbor. (Which isn't an entirely necessary rule, considering you wouldn't leave the harbor if you were lucky enough to be in it.) I've never seen the full storm flag on the Coast Guard Station. I'm wishing I could see it.

We get up a few more times to listen to the U.S. Weather Service acknowledge full storm warnings, and Charlie comes on the radio. He says the wind just blew the top off his wind gauge at 80 knots and twisted the cable. He says he is going in.

Hearing him say 80-knot winds triggers a memory I have of reading a book about heavy weather sailing. It mentioned 80-knot winds, and I think it said something like, "Large ships hug the shore, and small boats perish." This is not a comforting thought.

We would head in with Charlie except that with full storm warnings 200 miles away, going in doesn't sound encouraging. Old Flint finally says we'll have to go in if the storm continues to pick up. He mentions it isn't likely, since he has never seen anything like it before. I think he says that for reassurance, for me or for himself, because that makes it sound like going in is a solution. The swells are hitting the boat pretty bad--enough to consider firing up the engine. We're lying in our bunks thinking we'll have to do something pretty soon.

We could cut down the pounding on the boat if we turned into the sea and headed into it with the engine at moderate RPM. That would reduce the strain on the boat. I think the reason he hasn't done that is because he doesn't want to acknowledge that things are that desperate. A fisherman almost never turns and heads into the storm, because if it's that bad it's time to think of something else-- like heading in and looking for a point of land to hide behind. But he's considering it, because 200 miles off Blanco is like 200 miles off nowhere. It's the Oregon coast's Cape Horn. It's a long way to anything to hide behind.

Ollie asks me a couple of times what I think we should do, whenever another boat starts to head in. I refrain from expressing my opinion. He just asks me to see if I agree with him, which I would if he pushed me for a yes or no. He's a good seaman and knows what his boat will take. But it doesn't matter to me what he does; there isn't any good choice.

I'm a little wistful for Rudy's red wine and rollicking laughter to sort of take the edge off the terror. But I wouldn't trade the company for Rudy's shallow, 35-footer in this sea.

In the middle of the night, both of us are just listening to the creaking and straining of the boat, alert for any unusual noises. We're in our bunks trying to get some rest, because there isn't anything else we can do. But even if we had been asleep, we would have heard that thunderous crash. It was loud like a sonic boom, like something hit the boat. The boat shuddered, and everything on it creaked and strained and cracked. Whatever it was, it was a heavy blow.

Our bunks are in the fo'c'sle, so we have a minute or two on the way to the deck to imagine what that big bang was. The forecastle, or fo'c'sle, is the forward-most portion of living quarters on a boat, all the way up in the bow. The term fo'c'sle isn't used much anymore, because most modern boats have their water tank or fuel tanks there, or the engine that far forward to make room for their ice. But we had a fo'c'sle; we slept with our engine.

It's likely that the boat is breaking up--that's what we're thinking--but there are some other things it could be. Like a drifting log. We see those once in a while in the daytime, and you can't watch for them 24 hours a day. You could run into one of those clear out in albacore waters. That's often the speculation when a boat simply disappears during the night and is never heard from again. Another possibility is that another boat has hit us, and we're expecting to see a tangle of poles. There is a fair chance of another boat drifting into us in a sea like this.

They don't shut down within two miles of you, but that can be too close. Sometimes one will get into an unusual current and drift five miles farther than anybody else during a normal night--which this isn't. That's one of the other possibilities.

As we run up on deck to see what is demolished or what is missing, we're thinking in terms of the mast, or poles, or both. We have those 60-foot poles, outriggers, that we use for both salmon and albacore. For salmon the poles have stabilizers attached to them, but they would slow us down too much for albacore so they are secured on board. Noyo fishermen call them "flopper stoppers", and on a calm night we'd put them in the water to steady the boat, but in this sea there's too much risk of them hitting the side. We don't have them out in this weather.

When we see what it is, there's some relief to our anxiety. What has happened is serious, but not hopeless. A wave has broken over the side and hit the steady sail about dead center. With all the guy wires from the poles, and the standing rigging attached to the mast, it is like one solid unit with the boat; very rigid, not at all flexible. So when the wave hit it, it was just as if a solid object had hit the boat. It was immediately apparent what had happened, because it had completely covered the deck with water when it hit, and even after we got up there it was still completely covered. It wasn't white water, it was green water; not mist, a wave. It hit the side of the cabin too, but that didn't shake the boat as bad as hitting the sail.

When that happens, if the water doesn't run off fast enough it can take the boat over. The next wave might put it down forever. This boat has a severe crown to the deck, so much so that walking to port or starboard, in either direction from the center of the boat, you can actually tell you are walking downhill. The design of the boat is close to a full circle, which is what makes the boat so strong. I'm thinking about that crown to the deck, and how fast the water can run off, and trying not to think about the vulnerable midsection where the next wave might hit if the boat doesn't right itself before the next wave comes.

It is unusual, but not alarming, for the boat to lean enough to take water in the ice hold, which has a 2-foot coaming rim above deck level to keep waves from splashing in. It's nailed shut now, so we aren't in danger of taking water in the ice hold, but we're leaning like a sailboat. The strength of the boat is like an egg, as long as it is intact and the forces are equal. A strong wave over the side could break the rail off and still not sink us, because there is a strong junction where the deck beams meet the ribs. But if another wave of that force hits us while we're still down, it will hit right in the middle of the ribs. So, how fast the boat can right itself will determine whether it comes back at all.

We have to get that sail down, fast.

We have to fire up the engine. We can never get the sail down with that kind of wind pressure against it. My heart is in my throat. This is fun--action. This should happen every day. It gets the adrenaline going. You could do anything. I don't think Ollie is thinking this as he starts the engine, but he's movin'. Being on deck in this storm is exciting.

It's also extremely dangerous. There's a big risk of being washed overboard, and any yachtsman would be wearing a harness. When you consider that waves like this can knock the cabin off a steel boat, we're a little foolhardy to think we can hold on. Fishermen don't think like sailors. To begin with, a fisherman thinks nothing on a sailboat is heavy enough. He puts a lot more confidence in brute strength, including his own. A fisherman will tie on a line if he has to be on deck alone, but resists it for the same reason a lot of us resisted seat belts in cars. You think, am I protecting myself or trapping myself? It's irrational, but we prefer one risk to the other. We're hoping to get positioned so we can get the sail down and get back in the cabin before anything else hits.

There had been three other boats in view, off and on, when we shut down for the night. When we got on deck, we saw something else spooky. We looked around and saw no other mast lights. Most of the rest of the fleet, except for a couple of boats, had been running for about two hours toward the beach. They couldn't be making much progress, because you can't run even half speed in this kind of sea and still control the boat. And a top speed of 10 knots (12 mph) is impressively fast for a fishing boat.

We had slipped on our oilskins and our "fishermen's Romeos"--just slippers with heavy soles, high enough to keep your feet dry in normal conditions. (Romeos is the brand name.) They have no heels, just high soles and elastic sides. Fishermen use them because they're quick to slip into after taking off your boots if you have to go back on deck. When you stop fishing at eight at night after fishing all day, minutes count between dinner and bed. I'm wishing I had my boots on. There is some danger of filling them in this kind of weather, but this is definitely a time for boots, and I'm aware of it every time I try to find someplace to put my feet where they will stay with the deck awash. Every time my feet go out from under me, all my strength goes to holding myself steady with my arms. We're getting drenched, even with oilskins, but they keep the chill out. It's raining some, but most of the water is coming over the side.

We have to head directly into the wind to keep any more water from hitting the sail and to take the strain off the boat. It will take both of us to drop the sail and tie it down, which doesn't leave anybody to steer. So we have to turn the boat in the direction of the wind and then put it on automatic pilot, which is risky. The automatic pilots commonly found on small boats--and on this one--don't respond to the helm fast enough for heavy weather. When it's this unpredictable, we always do our own steering. We are facing another adventure, but it probably won't be any worse than laying in the trough and waiting for disaster.

As soon as we turn, the difference is dramatic. There is much less strain on the boat, and for the moment the danger has passed. We keep heading into it ten minutes or so to see if the setting we put the automatic pilot on will keep us heading as close as possible to directly into the wind. You can't be sure until after it's on a heading for at least a few minutes.

It seems far milder now because of the heading. The fore and aft motion is much less violent than with the boat laying in the trough. But it's still a lot of action. I'm wishing it were daylight so I could take some unbelievable pictures with my rusty Instamatic. That would make Ollie testy at a time like this. It isn't an option, because we are operating on deck with two 100-watt light bulbs. That isn't adequate to see what we're doing, much less take pictures. We do everything in the shadows, by feel. Lights aren't important on this boat, since you don't fish salmon and albacore at night. On a drag boat we would have quartz iodine flood lights a foot square. Those would be handy right now for getting the sail down--if we could see through the spray.

It is more than challenging, fighting hurricane-force winds to subdue a flapping sail. While we try to get it down, the wind keeps whipping it out of our hands. We have to furl it as it comes down so the whole thing can be lashed down on top of the mast. It takes us quite a while, probably not as long as it seems. Probably about 20 minutes.

Once we get the sail tied down, we go back in to try to get a weather report to see if there's any sign of it letting up. We don't expect to learn much, since the reports for the last three days have considerably underrated this storm. They generalize for the area, and apparently we've been lucky enough to be right in the eye of it. The reports are still full storm warnings, 60 to 70 knot winds.

Neither of us has any thoughts at this point of trying to stick it out. Boats much larger than us prepared for 30-day trips have headed in. We hear on the radio that one boat has broken up during the night and three men are lost, presumed drowned. Debris was reported by another fishing boat. There was no search; the Coast Guard couldn't get a plane or a helicopter up. It broke up while they were asleep, undoubtedly, because they didn't even get a Mayday out. They probably heard a crash while they were in their bunks, like we did. You can't swim to the radio.

The wind still seems to be picking up, if that's possible. Now that we've decided to go in, the question is where. It depends on what direction we can run safely, and whatever harbor is not out of range.

We quickly decide that running south is not the answer, since that means running in a following sea. You look behind you and see frothy, monster waves coming at you. Nobody likes a following sea except maybe somebody with a death wish. Each swell takes the boat faster than it would go under its own power, and you lose all your steering. A breaking one would swamp the stern. The swells are about 40 to 50 feet, with an occasional large one bigger than that. Surfing on these would be a thrill, which is what we would be doing if we headed south.

A fishing boat behaves very differently from a surf board, which has approximately 1/10 keel and the rest for planing. Steering a surf board, all you have to do is move the other 9/10ths, and you can do that with your body. A fishing boat is mostly keel, with a very small rudder. Only the rudder can be maneuvered, and it steers from the rear. This causes the boat to handle a lot like a fork lift, and it's impossible to hold the boat steady, even down one breaker. The wave doesn't hit you perfectly straight, and once the boat begins to turn, correcting it is impossible. Especially when you can't increase your speed above the speed of the wave. Our maximum speed is about 10 knots. We don't want to be quite that completely at its mercy if we can help it. That means we can't go to Shelter Cove, which sounds like about the best place to be, since the swells are coming from the northwest.

Quartering the swells downhill would be the next consideration, if it wasn't too bad. We decide that would be just as risky in this severe a sea. We could steer better, but with the boat speed combined with the speed of the swells, if one hit us it would knock us over just as bad as when we were laying dead in the trough with the sail up.

Running in the trough is out of the question: it's just too awesome. Green water on both sides of you as high as a 6-story building. You don't shoot the pipeline in a 45-foot boat--at least not this kid. I would argue about that one; but Ollie doesn't even think about it. That means we can't go into Coos Bay, which is the nearest harbor. Just looking in that direction you can picture yourself being swallowed up. You think, I'm okay, as long as I don't turn that way.

That leaves uphill, and quartering uphill. The problem is finding a place to go that isn't out of range. Looking at the charts, the only feasible place is to head for the Columbia River. That means Astoria to fishermen, although Astoria is upriver. You like a familiar port, and Ollie hasn't been into the Columbia for two years. Naturally, we are thinking in terms of what we can do, not what we might prefer. (By our standards, Ollie and I are getting almost sociable.)

The Columbia River Bar is one of the roughest areas in the world. Unobstructed waves from 3500 miles away meet the strong outgoing current of the river, and when you enter it waves are coming at you from three different directions. Compared with what we're in now, that doesn't even seem intimidating.

When we decide to run, we also decide that neither of us is to go on deck again alone. Normally, if something breaks loose in the stern, you go out and tie it down. But the motion of the boat is so violent, we decide no one will go on deck without the other standing in the doorway of the cabin, facing aft. If one is at the wheel, he won't know if the other is in trouble in time to do him any good. Before we start, we close and bolt the cabin doors. We have never done that before, and we've seen some heavy weather. It's the little things like that, nailing down the hatches, bolting the cabin door, that make this storm ominous.

One of the good things about a fisherman is that he never talks about how scary it is, no matter what's happening. You can be thinking there's only a slim chance you're going to make it, but you focus on that chance and do whatever you can. You can be scared as hell, but you don't admit it even to yourself, and never to the other guy. Some of them might, but I've never fished with anyone who did. You appreciate it, and with a taciturn man like Ollie, you're confident of it. You always know that whatever happens, nobody is going to panic. If there's anything you can do, both of you will do it. The odds are bad enough when it's you against nature; you don't compound the problem by letting fear control you. Good company might make it more pleasant, but in a situation like this, Ollie is my idea of good company.

After the other boat breaking up, bolting the cabin door is the grimmest thing that has happened so far. The only reason for doing that is to eliminate the danger of taking on water if the boat gets knocked down. It was clearly indicated, looking out those windows.

The Helga II has half-inch plate glass windows in Honduras mahogany frames, and half-inch plexiglass outside to form double windows. They built them right in those days. They are small windows by today's standards, but there is plenty of visibility. I don't think anything could knock out those windows, so that's one thing we don't have to worry about. Even so, I flinch whenever a wave hits them, expecting them to break any minute.

The only thing we have to settle now is how fast we might be able to run. It's a matter of trial and error, and the errors give us some of our wildest moments yet. Certain speeds set up a bucking motion because of the length of the boat and the length of the swell, and send the bow directly into an oncoming wall of green water. Suddenly it's blacker than it should be, and you look up and see no sky, just a wall of water. Your first instinct is to duck and grab something. You put your foot against the opposite wall, so if the boat goes over on its side, you're still standing up. You're thinking it's easier to run out of the cabin than to crawl out; not consciously, but that's why you're doing it. The stern is sunk in the trough, the boat pitches, and green water goes over the top of the cabin--<u>well</u> over the top of the cabin. The motion defies you to take enough steps forward and backward to maintain your balance, if you overcome the impulse to duck and grab. There's some motivation to try to keep steering, and it's a challenge to keep your attention on it.

Whichever one of us has the wheel does, because the other expects it.

Other types of motion we could take, like just pitching, but the forward and backward motion, along with the side-to-side motion you always get in this round-bottomed boat, were almost more than we could handle. It's like a carnival ride gone berserk, and you wish you could get off. Before we get the speed right, there is some challenging motion that isn't any easier on the boat than it is on us. You want to make things as easy as you can on the boat, because that's all you've got out there. Every unusual creak, you think, Come on, Baby, hold together.

The spookiest part of the bucking is when the boat comes off the swell and just lays there quiet, and then pitches suddenly forward. I don't know if the boat moves, or the wave comes to us, but then we really hear some unusual creaks and crackling noises. The maximum comfortable speed turns out to be about one-fourth of normal moderate weather running speed, about salmon trolling speed.

After a couple of waves broke clear over the house when we first tried to run too fast, we're speculating about whether the life preserver pod is still on top of the cabin, but we don't want to go out and look. We talk about it, just casually wondering. They aren't secured too well, because they have to be able to blast themselves off and free of the rigging if the boat does go over. His was the exploding pod variety, which is designed to blast off if the cartridge gets wet. He was a little concerned with the cost, about $800 then. It was a 6-man raft. Even though there are usually only two or three men on a boat, almost all of them have bigger rafts. I guess they figure the bigger, the better. There is also some pride involved. If you bought a 2-man raft, the other fishermen would give you a lot of flack, or just look at it and think, "Cheap son-of-a-bitch." There are a few things you don't do for no better reason than that.

I kind of hoped he hadn't lost his money, but I didn't care if it was there or not. We weren't considering it for its uses. We might have tried it as a last-ditch chance, but looking at that sea it was ridiculous to contemplate being out there in a raft. You'd die, simply from fright. It would go skipping around like a frisbee. Under different circumstances, like sitting in the bar at Bodega, we might have giggled at the thought.

At about daylight we hear a couple of boats on the radio that are almost all the way in. They say the weather has subsided quite a lot inside, and the Columbia River Bar isn't as bad as most of us had expected it to be. With the wind that high, we expected it to be impossible. There was even some question in our minds about whether to attempt to go in once we got there. Once we're into the beach, we can run back down to the nearest anchorage. When we are that far inside, there's enough protection from Tilamook Head to run downhill.

We think we're alone out here, and then we see a Japanese whaler about 150 feet long going around the cape. She's bucking into it, heading for Vancouver. They're taking green water over the bow and clear over the top of the ship. We can see the whole ship shudder every time they hit one, and the bow is buried for a few minutes. They aren't in any trouble. The swells are well spaced and pretty consistent, down to about 20 feet now. There's nobody on deck, but it looks like things are under control.

The sea eases up gradually as we get within about 25 miles of shore, and it gets progressively better. Ordinarily, this heavy chop and whitecaps would have been something to worry about, but now it seems like nothing. I'm thinking with amusement that if we had been in, Ollie would never have gone out in this. Now he's running full speed in a 6-foot chop, making the boat look something like a submarine. There's a constant shower of spray over the cabin, obliterating the boat. Spray, however; not green water. Now and then there's a little green water over the windows, but not clear over the cabin.

When we finally get close to shore, we run into a pea soup fog bank for a few miles, and we're constantly watching the radar for other boats. We can't see anything. The fog bank is a surprise, because there was so much wind where we were, we never expected to run into a windless area. Then we hear on the radio that it's crystal clear and the sun is shining when you get within two miles of the beach. We're relieved to hear that, because going into an unfamiliar harbor with charts and radar alone is something you dread. We've just about used up all our adrenaline, and we're looking forward to a comforting bar.

Ollie unbolts the cabin door after we are clear inside, and says the life raft is still there. It has taken us just about 12 hours to get here, and it's a relief to come out of the fog bank and see that sunshine, even though it is still choppy. We don't have the stamina to negotiate with ships for our part of the channel in the fog. There's nothing but a traffic light at the entrance to the Columbia, and it's green for entry. There are still full storm warnings, and everybody is coming in; nothing is going out.

Ollie says, "Let's get a beer." That's the closest we come to becoming buddies. We aren't feeling jovial, because we haven't made any money, but there is less tension between us.

After everybody is accounted for that made it in, we learn that three other boats from our fleet were lost in this storm, besides the first one that broke up. We tried to believe they might turn up in other ports; everybody made their own decisions about when to go in and where to head. But we were not surprised when they were never found. We all were looking at the same conditions, and Astoria was the only real option.

This was a "survival storm", which means that wind and sea have taken control, and the course is dictated by the need to take the breaking waves at the best angle. In that kind of storm, you go wherever it lets you, and just try to stay afloat. Any one of us could as easily have capsized as survived. Nobody who made it was congratulating himself, except maybe on his luck.

We all call our wives and girlfriends and tell them we were 200 miles out and we missed the storm. It was a little choppy, and the fishing wasn't good, but we're fine. No use worrying them. It's better to let them think the lost boats were off together away from the fleet and ran into some bad weather. They do compare notes, but nobody tells them anything scary because it only gives them a reason to be down on fishing. This was an exceptional storm.

Vi was glad to hear from me. Our house is close to the ocean about two miles south of Noyo. We can't hear the fog horn or the buoys from our house when the sea is calm; the motion of the waves rocks the buoy and sounds the bell. During this storm she was lying in bed at night listening to the bell buoy clanging and the fog horn blowing, and she was scared thinking of me out there in the storm. There were full storm warnings all the way to Fort Bragg.

We go to the noisiest bar we can find. After you're out fishing for a week or more and you haven't seen anyone else but whoever you're fishing with, you want to see people. The more there are, the better you like it. It doesn't matter what they're doing. We don't get impatient watching any kind of behavior. We're just happy to be alive, and reminded that there are other people in the world. This is the remarkable day I get to see Ollie smile.

We're sitting at a table near the bar having a beer. There are two guys standing between the bar and the tables, having a slow-motion altercation. It goes on interminably. They're both fairly young, late twenties, both medium height and slight build, and both very drunk. One of them gives the other one a wimpy push, carefully steadying himself first with his feet wide apart so he won't fall down. The other one manages to stay standing, composes himself, gradually screws his face up to an affronted look, and prepares to return the blow. Then he delivers a similar push to his adversary, looks self-satisfied, and stands back bracing for the next round. This goes on for at least fifteen minutes. We lose interest and look away. When we look back, they're always still bravely doing battle, with no signs of either one giving up, ever. Then I see it: Ollie's mouth is curving up ever so slightly. It's a smile.

For the rest of the season, Ollie is a lot less cautious about when to go out. Even if we go out in a chop, we aren't likely to get into anything quite like that again. He stops sweating the small stuff. Even so, I decide that life is too short to fish with Old Flint for more than one season. He isn't making us much money, and there's no other good reason for spending time with him. I plan to be on a different boat next year, and will take the skipper's attitude and disposition into account when I pick it.

CHAPTER 8

DRAGGING THE DEPTHS

Trawling the bottom on a drag boat, or trawler, has all the drudgery of any physical 8 to 12-hour-a-day job. You drag a net on the bottom and scoop up fish so far below that it's always night for them. It's a day and night routine, with most of the fun taken out of fishing. It's better than a job on land, because the elements still make it exciting, but I'd rather be trolling.

Spring 1975

I put out the word at Noyo and tell everyone I know that I'm looking for a job on some other boat. There's a drag boat that might have a spot opening up. The skipper is Ted Winthrop, one of the fishermen I met working for Tony on the docks. He was an architect who left it for fishing. He says he might need another crewman, but not for a few weeks. He tells me to check back with him later. What both of us don't know is that in a few weeks he's going to need a new boat.

About the time I start thinking about looking up Ted again, I hear that his drag boat ran into the rocks just north of the harbor entrance. There was some heavy weather so they couldn't get in. They decided to run back and forth in front of the harbor to wait, because it's more comfortable to run than to sit there in a rough sea in that boat. They always have plenty of fuel, and the rest of the crew can get some sleep while one of them steers.

The crewman at the wheel wasn't watching for the east and west drift as he ran back and forth, so he ran them into the beach on his next pass north. They were a little off shore, and there could have been strong currents or big swells. They have radar, and the radar screen is right in front of you, so there's not much excuse for not looking at it. If he had, he would have seen the point out in front of him, instead of off to the side of him. It's boring running up and down, and he was obviously not paying attention, if not actually asleep.

The Coast Guard picked them up and everybody made it out okay. The boat was a 65 foot steel boat with a 1/4 inch steel plate hull and a 10-gauge metal house, but it was badly damaged. They were all pretty shaken up, and Ted Winthrop was very upset about his boat, but glad all of them survived it. He was just starting to make a profit, and his wife, who thought she married an architect, was just beginning to accept his new career. He didn't need this, and it shouldn't have happened, so he was not taking it very well.

I went to see him anyway, at Noyo, where he was looking over what was left of the boat to see what he could salvage. It wasn't much. The damage was about $125,000 and the entire cost of the boat was $160,000, not including electronics. Those were $70,000 and were not damaged.

Ted asked me if I had ever done any welding. Since I had, he sent me to see Larry, the owner of the boat yard that was doing the repair work on his boat. He said Larry had a welder, but needed a fitter to work with him. Ted wouldn't commit about a job on the boat, but he said to talk to Larry about a job getting his boat fixed, and we'd see about that later.

I got the job with Larry as a fitter for the boat yard, and worked on Ted's boat and a couple of other boats that were being repaired. Ted's boat wasn't getting finished fast enough for him, and he began to suspect that the boat yard was diverting the workers to four other boats they were working on, delaying his deliberately and trying to get more money out of his insurance company. One day Ted met me getting off work and said he wanted to talk to me away from Noyo, so I met him later at a coffee shop in town.

He said he had arranged with his insurance company to finish the repairs himself, and he was going to move the boat off the boat yard's property that night. He had arranged for a place to keep it and work on it just across the property line, so he only had to move it about 100 feet. He was afraid if he told the boat yard in advance, they would delay it and wouldn't give him access to his boat. He wanted me to quit my job, and take over as foreman for him to get his boat finished. He offered me a couple of dollars more an hour than I was getting from the boat yard.

If I did that, I would be burning some bridges. I had a pretty good job with the boat yard, and I wouldn't have a job at all when his boat was finished. So I told him I would do it on the condition that when the boat goes in the water, I go with it. He agreed to that. A couple of the other people he had originally sent to work at the boat yard made similar deals, so he already had a crew for the boat repairs. That night we helped the movers use house moving equipment to move the boat off the boat yard property.

Ted had been drag fishing with that boat long enough to know what he didn't like about it and what could be improved. It didn't take long for him to turn the disaster into an opportunity. He was an architect, and he had some innovative ideas.

Drag boats always had a reel, but nobody ever thought of building a double one. There was always an extra net ready to go, but they used the same net until it got torn. Ted designed a double reel, so at the end of a tow you could haul in the net, unhook it and hook it onto the other reel, and put the other net out right away. That saves an hour and a half between tows, and you have a net in the water practically all the time. He was the first at Noyo to equip his drag boat that way, and now everyone does.

The boat was almost completely rebuilt, so Ted had the opportunity to make some major changes. It's easy to do innovative things with a steel boat; you just weld it on. With a wooden boat, if you're bolting something to a plank you can't put too much strain on one plank; you have to spread it over a wider area.

Ted wasn't a naval architect, but being an architect gave him an understanding of what it was safe to tamper with and still keep the boat structurally sound. He made a lot of modifications that improved the size and stability of the work deck. He also gave it a more convenient layout for the winches and for sorting and handling fish. His biggest overall consideration was its capacity for holding fish; that came right after survivability, which was the primary design goal in the boat's original design.

Joshua Slocum completely rebuilt the Spray in 1892 for his trip around the world, yet it remained the Spray, when there was hardly anything left of the old boat. He commented, "It is a law in Lloyd's that the Jane repaired all out of the old until she is entirely new is still the Jane."[2] It's still more trouble than it's worth to change the name of a documented vessel registered worldwide, and the Big Dipper kept her name, even though she was nearly a whole different boat.

This diversion from my fishing career gives me some common ground with my dad, a saw filer who does welding in his job. He can relate to this job much better than to fishing for a living. My mother can, too. She had her sights on college for me, and eventually President, but now she thinks cooking or welding would both be fine careers. Their goals for me are now simplified to anything except fishing. Vi is pleased about it too, because we're expecting a baby in a few months, but it turns out that I don't get to spend much time at home.

Ted is impatient to finish his boat so he can start fishing and recover financially. The drag boats have been doing exceptionally well this season. We're getting close, but he keeps pushing us for longer hours. I'll be glad when it's done so we can get back to working a 10 or 12-hour day.

---

[2]Slocum, Joshua Sailing Alone Around the World; W. W. Norton & Company, New York, London, 1984; p. 5

There's another steel boat being built next to Ted's that is using an employment training program for labor, and they don't seem to have adequate supervision. The welder and I went over to look at it, and he noticed they were measuring from the hull instead of the water line to put in the deck. That would have been interesting on launching day. He alerted the owner, and I guess that got fixed, but I'm glad I'm not going to fish on that boat. It's progressing so slowly, it doesn't look like they are going to finish it during the owner's lifetime, so he's probably safe.

Even though Ted isn't superstitious, we still do the traditional things, like putting a coin under the mast. We're breaking a bottle of champagne on the bow. Why take chances?

After about three months, two weeks after our son Brian is born, the Big Dipper is finally ready to launch. It doesn't take long to get it in the water. The boat is already on housemover wheels, and four large semi-type tow trucks get it on the ramp. There's always a little anticipation at a boat launching. You're hoping that when it breaks the crest of the ramp, it doesn't pull the trucks into the water. You're hoping that it floats. Irrational things like that. It's in the water in about an hour, and it floats. It's riding high in the water, because it doesn't have its ballast yet. The cement trucks are scheduled for tomorrow.

We need a tow boat to take it to the fitting out dock, and our tug is the Helga II. Ted knows Ollie, just by coincidence. Ollie is an incredible boat handler, and his boat is big enough to move the Big Dipper. He could tie up to a big boat like that and maneuver it around in the harbor without damaging it; not everybody could. But there are quite a few others with big enough boats who could have done it; Ollie just happened to be around. I don't have a big role in the launching, so it isn't too awkward. Let's just say we skip the tearful reunion. I think the way we left it when I departed the Helga II was that we respected and hated each other. That's not a big liability among fishermen, because there's not a whole lot of social interaction.

Ted is impatient to go fishing, but there are still a few things to do before we can take the boat out. Concrete has to be poured into compartments below the floor boards in sort of a grid, leaving a shaft alley for the propeller shaft. It takes 10 yards or more of concrete to provide this ballast about three feet deep in the bottom of the boat. Then the engine and electronic gear can be installed while it sets up for a day. We'll be able to take a trial run the next day.

One of Ted's friends, a school teacher, has been spending a lot of time helping with the repair work, fetching things for us and serving as an errand person for whatever we needed while we were working on the boat. Ted promised Bill a boat ride when it was finished, so he goes with us on the trial run. We're not ready to fish yet, and we still have welding equipment all over the boat, just in case we need to repair something. The run today is just to make sure everything works and to see what we've overlooked. We have to secure drawers and all the incidental items that bump and rattle when the boat goes out on the rolling ocean.

We planned to go out a little farther, but Bill finds out that he is not a sailor after all, so we cut it short to just four or five passes in front of the harbor. That's plenty of time for Bill to have all the experience he wants on the ocean.

I was expecting a break for a few days before we were ready to go fishing, but Ted has expedited everything he could so he would be all prepared when it hit the water. All he needs now is fuel and ice. We're going out to fish tomorrow for three days. Ted has some crew members coming to rig the nets tonight, and he has done the shopping already.

Early in the morning we're on our way to the fishing grounds. This is my first time on a steel boat, and Rudy is right; it doesn't feel like a wooden boat. The engine sounds different, resounding against the metal. The feel riding on the water is not nearly as smooth. Some people will tell you that it's sentiment that makes you like a wooden boat and resist steel. Don't believe them. This boat has a lot of nice features the wooden boats I've been on didn't have, like hydraulic steering so the wheel doesn't overpower you, and it has all the luxury of the St. Jude (or a Class A motor home), but it rides like a D-8 Caterpillar. It doesn't glide naturally through the water; it's more like lurching. You feel like you're getting on a big tractor, riding it around for three days, and then coming back and parking it.

If you're used to a wooden boat, and then have to adapt to a steel one, the hardest thing to get used to is the difference in the sounds, even more than the feel of the ride. A gust of strong wind will cause reverberations in the metal that turn the whole boat into a guitar, and you'll hear some bizarre music you never heard in a wooden boat. You get used to it, but it gives stormy weather a soundtrack that keeps you on edge. In a ferocious storm, it can sound like a pipe organ gone crazy.

Having established that there are some real and significant aesthetic advantages to a wooden boat, the sentimental attachment to them and the blatant practicality of the steel boats replacing them at Noyo appears in a different light. What is happening here in the fishing industry is just another industrial revolution, another technological advance that makes the old, comfortable ways obsolete.

To most Noyo fishermen, wooden boats feel more like home, and they like the pride and skill of capturing fish fairly and knowing that enough of them always escape to assure the continued health of the fishery. Most of the fishermen don't welcome the new electronics for fish finding, or the larger steel boats. What is worse for them than rendering their boats and methods obsolete is the fact that the changes make their unique skills worthless. They get the new boats and the new equipment because they have to if they are to stay competitive. But these changes are taking a lot of the joy out of fishing. Even Killer Willie doesn't like them, but he's adjusting to them a lot better than his colleagues with Makela brothers boats, who will never give them up.

A master fisherman can still earn a good living with a well constructed wooden boat. No one who has one is getting rid of it, because they are virtually irreplaceable. The cost is now prohibitive, and the craftsmen capable of building one are few. Even if money were no object, it might be several years before a wooden boat could be commissioned to be built. Then the building would take a year, or at least a season.

A well built wooden boat, if taken care of, will last a hundred years. A steel boat is much cheaper to build, and it will last 25 or 30 years. A wooden boat is a valuable family business. A steel boat is just farm machinery. So, yes, there is a lot of sentiment involved too. It just shouldn't be confused with an appreciation for the true superiority of wood and its properties for floating on the water, and for making the natural sounds you're supposed to hear at sea.

Drag fishing is new to me, so I have to learn to handle the gear. It's pretty simple compared with salmon gear. The hard part is maintaining the right speed when you're dragging the net. Trolling for salmon is done at a moderate speed that makes the bait look natural as it moves in the water. Trawling for bottom fish with large nets is done at a slower speed. You have to make sure not to move too slowly, because iron doors keep the net spread apart and down, and if you aren't moving enough, the net will dig deeper and deeper into the mud at the bottom. Eventually, it can get to the point where the winch on the boat won't lift it.

It's hard to tell whether you're moving. If the current below you is moving just as fast as you are, you aren't moving when you think you are. The only way to be sure is to take loran readings every fifteen minutes to see how far you've traveled. Loran has improved a lot over the last ten years since I started fishing, and it's much easier to use and more reliable. That's part of watch duty, and someone is on watch all the time when the net is in the water.

On the Big Dipper, we fish day and night. In the daytime we fish in relatively shallow water where the bottom is sandy, and catch mainly rock cod, ling cod, black cod, and five different species of sole. At night we fish for Dover sole in about 60 fathoms, so deep that day or night doesn't matter. During the times of the year when you don't catch cod, we do all our fishing in deep water. We have a mile of cable on the winches.

You know what's on the bottom, because you get some of all of it--whatever is there. We usually catch what we're expecting, but once in a while there's something strange in the net. On our second trip out we catch a transparent fish that has a backbone, but looks more like an eel than a fish. Nobody has ever seen anything like it, so we give it to a marine biologist stationed at Noyo who does fish inspections. We never hear what it is, or if anybody knows.

On another trip we catch a big airplane wing, and have to bring it all the way onto the boat to get it free of the net. We report its position and identifying numbers to the Coast Guard, in case it is still among their unsolved mysteries.

The airplane wing was a logistical problem, but we run into an even bigger one when we catch the funnel from a big ship. It weighs a couple of tons, and we have to bring it on board in heavy weather. We have to cut the net to get it out, and then we finally get it hoisted over the side with the boom winches.

The most unusual marine creature we caught was a 15-foot giant squid. It was tangled in the net and came up from about 60 fathoms, so it was dead on arrival at the top, but it was a magnificent specimen. We had only heard about those; I wasn't even sure I believed they existed. Not many fishermen have seen them, and not much is known about them. They're usually the subjects of "monster from the deep" movies. We gave that to the marine biologist too. He had seen some, but none that big. It's head was about three feet long, with eyes as big as baseballs, and the tentacles were about 10 or 12 feet long. It was pretty impressive. If it had been alive, it could have grabbed us all.

Sometimes we would catch strange little fish 6 to 8 inches long with sharp teeth as long as their bodies. Those were extremely unusual too, and we gave them to the marine biologist. He never got back to us about anything. I don't know why we bothered giving things to him. He was a personable guy, and was friendly with the Coast Guard and some of the other fishermen. He looked at us like we were scum. He didn't approve of trawling. Some people thought it was destroying the marine environment, but I think they must have been talking about boats a lot bigger than ours, and a lot more of them than there were at Noyo. We couldn't be making much of an impression on the marine environment with the range of it we could cover. He should go out with us some time and get a feel for how big the ocean is, and how little we are.

Fishing around the clock is a new experience for me, because you don't catch salmon and albacore at night. Drag fishing turns out to be the closest thing to an 8 to 5 job on land, because of the regular schedule. It takes three days to fill the boat with fish. Then you come in, unload it, get more fuel and ice, and go back out the next day and do it again. If there are net repairs, you might stay in an extra day, but Ted has an extra net to substitute so he doesn't lose any time. He's trying to make up for his loss in one year, so we're on a killer schedule.

We still have fun. There's more joking around, because it's a bigger crew. We play tricks on each other, and entertain the tourists coming and going. Jeff is the biggest cut-up. When we're coming in and he sees people on the dock, he'll pick up a shark as big as he is and pretend he's fighting it for his life. It's dead, of course, but he tries to make it look fierce. He's doing it to make us laugh, so when the tourists laugh that's okay too.

After a bad storm, Ted was anxious to make up for lost time. When the weather was coming down we would fudge by a day or so and go out when the sea was still rough and waves were breaking over the jetty, before anybody else was even thinking of going out.

That was exciting. We would be blasting out of the harbor at full throttle between the jetties, because the boat was capable of it. It takes a lot of power to plow through the breaking surf, but we had a huge motor and huge propellers. We had a GMC V-12, a diesel that would power a locomotive without much trouble. If there was anybody on the jetty to show off for, it was even more fun. It got their attention when they were standing on a two thousand pound granite boulder, and it was vibrating from something going by in the water. It looked and felt like sailing off the end of the world. Maybe we were, if it didn't come down. We wouldn't get back in until it did.

A steel boat will take that kind of a pounding. You don't have to worry about structural integrity, but you wouldn't do that in a wooden boat.

Some fishermen are conservative and never take these risks. Others are hustlers and always do, to get an edge. It's important for the crew members to share the skipper's inclination about it, or there is friction. If the skipper hires the crew, that happens naturally. You know the skipper's reputation when you hire on. But it's not always a compatible mix when it's a family boat. Fathers and sons sometimes differ in their attitudes about risk, and brothers often do. Some of them can only work it out by getting their own boat if the difference is too great.

In our case, we signed on with a cautious skipper and got the opposite. I didn't mind, because I'm a risk taker, but we had some crew changes before everybody was behind the skipper. There were six of us, and at the end of the season there were only two of us left from the original crew.

I liked Ted a lot better before he became so driven. He used to enjoy fishing, but now he seems to be drudging at it and losing interest in everything else. I think he will make up for his financial loss in one year. When he does, I hope he'll go back to the way he was before, but I'm beginning to wonder if he ever will. I'm trying to look at the positive side and enjoy making some money, but I wouldn't be out on the ocean all the time if I had a choice. With a baby at home, it would be nice to have a whole weekend break, or even a couple of days in the middle of the week.

I still like fishing, though, and even on a drag boat there is always something happening that you're not anticipating to keep it interesting.

Rescue of the Theresa S

Today it's the weather. It's rough, and the swells are about ten feet high. We've seen some bad weather on this boat, and the boat takes it pretty well. It's a solid boat, and it will take a lot before water starts coming over the side; but once it does, there's nothing you can do. It's like having someone throw rocks at you, and not being able to duck.

We're preparing to go in when we get a radio call from the Coast Guard. They have a Mayday from a yacht with eight people aboard, out about 20 miles. They also have a call from the Theresa S with a stalled engine off Cleone, near where we are. There are only three people on the Theresa S, so the other call takes priority. The Coast Guard asks us to go help them, because we're the closest boat.

We don't have a launch, and we can't risk getting very close to them in 10-foot swells. The Coast Guard asks us to try to get a line to them somehow and keep them off the rocks until they can return, and they continue on their way to respond to the other call.

If you are in the vicinity of someone who puts out a Mayday call, you are obligated to help them if you can without risking your own life. If you are the one putting out the Mayday call, you would prefer to have the Coast Guard respond, because they are much better equipped and trained to rescue you than another fishing boat. Their boats are faster and more powerful, and they have motor launches aboard, and crewmen trained in rescues. The trouble is, when conditions are bad enough that boats start to need rescuing, the first priority call is unlikely to be the small fishing boat with only two or three people aboard. So we are the only hope for the Theresa S to avoid going on the rocks, and we're not sure what we can do about it.

The Theresa S is an old, wooden drag boat that looks a lot like a shrimp boat, and is about the same size as the Big Dipper. When we get near Cleone, we see them rolling around in the breakers, helpless, and headed for the rocks. A few hundred yards and they won't be rolling around anymore; they'll be getting hammered.

We don't know how we're going to get a line to them, but we have to figure it out quickly. We move in as close as we dare. There are three men aboard. We can see their faces now, and they're scared.

The boat is riding about a foot below her water line.

This is a terrible feeling, worse than being in a storm and worried about yourself. Then it's just you to be concerned about. It's different to be looking at somebody else going into the rocks. You're okay, and you know they're gonna die if you can't do something fast. We don't have any equipment to use, or even a decent tow line except for a heavy cable. It's not that easy for one big drag boat to rescue another one that's disabled. You can't get very close together, because there's too much danger of the boats hitting each other if they're only one or two swells apart.

We try using a monkey's fist to throw them a line attached to a tow line. It's just a ball of line, like a tennis ball. In this wind, every time we throw it, it lands about 20 feet from us. It's too light. You can tell from the looks on their faces that our feeble tries haven't inspired their confidence. We know these guys. We don't want to watch them drown.

I go get a quart Clorox bottle and fill it with water. It weighs about two pounds, and should be heavy enough. We tie it to the line. I have to get clear of the rigging so I can swing it around my head. We don't have anything for a tow line except a very heavy cable that is usually pulled by a winch. Even if we can get the line to them, it's going to take incredible strength for them to pull the cable to their boat. But first things first. They're getting very close to the rocks.

The skipper gets our stern as close to them as he dares. Two 65-foot boats are very precarious only about 60 feet apart, only one swell apart in this sea. I climb to the top of the net reel and straddle it to get clear of the rigging. Jeff, another crewman, stands under the reel and holds my ankles so I can stay there in the wind without holding on. I need both hands free to swing the Clorox bottle over my head and toss it to the Theresa S. I tell Jeff not to let go.

The first try comes close, but misses. They look a little more hopeful. The next try is a little closer, but still out of their reach. There's only about enough time for one more try. This one breaks their cabin window, but they don't mind that a bit.

The three of them have to use all their muscles and adrenaline to budge that heavy cable, but they are strongly motivated. They are only a few feet from the rocks. They manage to get it there and secured, and the skipper gives us a signal. We start up and tow them out of danger, just in time.

We're all really feeling good now. The skipper and crew on the Theresa S have their lives back. We're only three miles from the harbor, so it's an easy tow home.

The skipper of the Theresa S wants us to tow them on into the harbor, but our skipper makes them wait for the Coast Guard. We don't have any way to secure them to us tight enough to make it safe for both boats to come in side by side under our power. We would both be taking a chance if they came in behind us with no power. They can safely anchor in the bay and wait. We're going to quit while we're ahead.

CHAPTER 9

MAYDAY

*If you believe in fate, believe in it,
at least, for your good.*
Emerson

This week everybody I knew at Noyo was walking around kicking rocks; the whole place was in a bad mood. The weather was gloomy, but it was more than that. Sam Conners had lost his new boat, and two of our friends were lost with it. Sam had quit fishing, and we were all bummed about it.

For some mysterious reason, it seemed that the ocean would not accept Sam on its surface, or even into its depths. He had finally come to believe there was some force working against his being a fisherman, and he gave it up for good, even though he didn't want to.

If you knew Sam Conners, or even saw him at Noyo, you would think he was born to fish. He loved the life, and looked like you'd expect a fisherman to look. He was big and muscular, with reddish hair, in his early thirties, good looking, and everybody liked him. He was a hard worker and a natural fisherman.

Sam started going out fishing summers when he was 8 years old, and when he graduated from high school he took his place as a regular crewman on his uncle's boat. He married his high school girlfriend, Charlene, and a couple of years later they bought a little, run-down place with a few acres in the pygmy forest south of Noyo. It was a nice country setting with lots of room for their two children to play, but in an area where the trees are stunted to about four feet tall, where nobody who wanted to grow anything would buy land, so it was cheap. They got Charlene a reliable car, and Sam drove a crummy car that might get you there and might not, and they began saving so he could buy his own boat.

He did well fishing, and Charlene didn't seem to mind taking most of the responsibility for the house and the children. Both of them had families close by, and a network of friends from their church, so she always had help when something needed fixed and he was out fishing. He was almost always out fishing or at Noyo working on the boat. He worked year around, fishing for salmon and albacore in the summer, and crab and bottom fish in the winter.

On the Mendocino coast, dungeness crab is an important treat for Christmas and New Year's celebrations. For me, crab is as much associated with Christmas as tinsel and holly. We don't have snow on this coast, but we nearly always have some dramatic wind and rain storms for the Christmas season. Sometimes we have to forego the cracked crab if the weather doesn't cooperate. But if it calms down at all, the crab fishermen try to supply plenty of crab.

Some time during the holidays you cover the table with thick layers of newspaper, put a cutting board and a hammer in the middle, and serve one crab for each person. With a loaf of sourdough French bread and some wine, that's dinner or a party. The more genteel supply each person with a nutcracker and a cocktail fork. It's important to have individual bowls of a good dip: either home made cocktail sauce (catsup, lemon juice, and a little Worcestershire and tabasco) or some mayonnaise mixed with lemon juice and a dash of mustard. The only thing better was when we could catch crabs off the Big River bridge and boil them on the beach. It's against the law now to hang crab pots off a bridge on the state highway.

I never eat crab without thinking of the dangers of crab fishing. It's done in the worst weather of the year, and under the most dangerous conditions. The crabs are on the bottom near the rocks, so the boats have to operate close to the rocks in turbulent seas. The crab pots are all on deck, stacked high, so the weight makes the boats top-heavy and more vulnerable to tipping over in a rough sea. It doesn't stop me from eating crab--they need the money-- but it makes me appreciate it more.

This year the crab season was late getting started, because the fishermen didn't like the price they were offered and refused to go out until they could negotiate a better price. There wasn't a very strong fishermen's organization at this time, but the fishermen were always united when they were not offered much more than a break-even price for crab. It was too dangerous to do for nothing, and in the sixties crab wasn't anybody's primary source of income. They could afford to hold out for a decent price, especially if they'd had a good salmon season. They all said, "I can't make anything at that price. I've got enough money in the bank; I think I'll stay home." When they finally got their price, there was a shortage of crab on the market and a big demand.

Sam and his uncle were among the first boats out when they got a break in the weather. If they hadn't been, they wouldn't have gone out at all. By the time other boats were ready to go, a new weather front had moved in and conditions were becoming serious for the boats already out. On Sam's boat, they had set out all the crab pots, and wanted to retrieve them before they tried to get back in. The winds were high, and the surf had kicked up to about 10-foot swells. Waves were breaking over the jetty.

They were picking up crab pots near the rocks when a breaking wave swamped the boat, and the engine died. Before they could get it started, they were pushed into the rocks. They grabbed life jackets, and one of them radioed a Mayday with their position before the boat broke up.

The Coast Guard heard their Mayday call late in the afternoon, a little before sundown. The boat was north of Mendocino, at Russian Gulch. At least they didn't have far to go to answer the call. They could be there in less than an hour. Conditions were not good for going out, and worse for coming back in, but psychologically it was a better time for a rescue in that weather than midnight would have been. At least the Coast Guardsmen were awake and ready to go. The cutter was plowing through the breaking waves between the jetties within about five minutes.

The estimated survival time in the water this time of year is about 45 minutes, but every fisherman knows it's probably longer than that if you're tough and have a little weight on you. The three fishermen on Sam's uncle's boat were all big, strong men. They were all in the water by the time the Coast Guard arrived, and Sam had retrieved the life raft after it blew clear of the wreckage, and was trying to pick up the other two. He wasn't having much success trying to paddle the raft against the force of the surging swells, and they weren't either in trying to swim toward it. They were all glad to see the Coast Guard.

By then it was dark, but the raft made it easier to spot them in their lights. The Coast Guard could see all three of them, and easily picked them up in their motorized rubber launch. Within about twenty minutes they were on the cutter getting warmed up with blankets, sips of brandy and hot coffee.

It is not unusual for the Noyo community to lose a boat or two in crab season, but it is not the norm for everyone on board to survive the sudden breakup of a boat after a Mayday call. There was an atmosphere of real joy and fellowship in Noyo and Fort Bragg this Christmas, crab or no crab. The Coast Guard crew was feeling festive too, even though some of them weren't getting home for the holidays.

His first time in the water caused Sam to rethink his fishing career a little, but he decided that the analogy about falling off a horse probably applied here too. The dangers were more real to him, but he always knew the possibility was there. They had all survived. It didn't change his outlook very much, except that he had a new awareness of the importance of providing for his wife and children. He resolved to get his own boat as soon as he could.

With their savings and a large mortgage, he bought a beautiful 55-foot boat that was in a category far superior to his house or car. He hired a crewman, and continued to have a successful fishing career for three years. Then one evening about dusk he told a friend on the radio that he was heading in when both of them were about six miles from the harbor. A storm had come up, and it was blowing about 30 knots. The wind was from the southwest, and the swells were reaching some alarming heights. His friend headed in soon after, and had an exciting time getting into the harbor. He got worried when Sam wasn't there when he got into port, so he called the Coast Guard, and they started a search.

By then it was dark and the wind was up to 40 knots and it was raining hard. The Coast Guard found some debris about a mile out, and on the way in they found Sam's life raft with no one in it. The local radio station had picked up the report of the missing boat, and a friend had called Charlene. By 10 p.m. everyone in Fort Bragg knew Sam and his crewman were missing, and that the Coast Guard had called off the search until morning. What they had found probably convinced them there was nothing to search for.

Normally, the locals accept the wisdom of the Coast Guard and don't question their decisions. This time it was different. Sam Conners was vitality personified; everybody who knew him believed that he was out there somewhere, alive. It wasn't inconceivable to Sam's friends that he would swim in from six miles out and walk up on the beach. At least they knew he would never give up, and they weren't having anyone give up on him this soon. They were determined that the search would go on through the night until they found him.

Phones started ringing all over the state. They called local officials, who called their Assemblyman and their Congressman at their homes; they called the radio station; they called TV stations in San Francisco and in Eureka; and they called the Coast Guard at Noyo and in San Francisco. The search was resumed.

About 2:00 a.m. the Coast Guard cutter picked up Sam Conners clinging to the bell buoy just outside the harbor. The buoy was rocking wildly in the swells, and he was pretty wet from the rain and the occasional wave breaking over him, but he had found a secure perch and locked his legs around the cross members of the triangular structure. It was like sitting on a big gyroscope, but it moved slower and more rhythmically. Sam was cold and exhausted, but still strong and alert. As soon as they got him in warm blankets, he was feeling pretty good.

He told them a freak wave had hit the cabin and the boat rolled over, and just kept going. It went down about three miles out.

There was nothing wrong with the boat; it was a good boat, deep enough for rough seas. It was just one of those erratic things that happens rarely, when all the circumstances are exactly right. Waves at sea don't always come in neat little rows, like they do on a long, unobstructed beach. They sometimes come from all directions, especially in a storm, and occasionally there is one much bigger than the rest. Once in a while one will break. The boat was positioned just right to get knocked over, the wave was unusually big, and it came from just the right angle.

There was no time to get a Mayday out. They didn't have life jackets on. The last time Sam saw his crewman, he was clinging to a steel crab tank that had been loose on deck. It's a liner that fits in the ice hold, all the way to the bottom, so it's about 8 feet long. It was the only thing floating that was big enough to hold onto, and it was only a matter of time until a wave would hit it from the open side, and it would fill and sink.

Sam was treading water. He had been through this before, and expected that the raft would blow clear eventually and come up, but so far it hadn't. He couldn't order his crewman to wait, on the off chance that it would; you're not skipper anymore when you're in the water. When the cylinder of the raft gets wet, it's supposed to explode and come to the surface. I can almost hear Louie saying, "That damn thing don't work." It was a very long time before the raft came up, and by then Louie, the crewman, was gone.

Sam eventually caught up with the raft, and stayed on it until he got to the buoy. Then he gave it up for the buoy, to avoid going into the rocks. It was not as cold on the buoy as it was in the water, but he was very chilled and tired by the time they picked him up. He knew if he could hold on, eventually someone would see him, even if it wasn't until morning. He got very tired of that loud clanging bell, but he was glad it was there. While he was waiting he got some good ideas for how buoys could be better designed for this purpose.

This wasn't the first time the Coast Guard had picked up a fisherman clinging to that buoy. There is a saying among fisherman that if you end up in the water, your chances for survival are better if you swim out than if you try to swim in. That may be hard to believe if you've never been swimming in the ocean, or tried to climb up on a slippery rock covered with seaweed, spiny sea urchins, and various slimy sea creatures while battling the surge of powerful waves. It's like being in a giant washing machine set for heavy duty. Even if you make it up onto a rock, the chances are you'll just be swept off again before you get rescued.

Even so, I've only known of one fisherman who ever actually did capsize and swim the opposite direction from shore. He was a huge man named Jeff Larson, who weighed about 300 pounds, and had plenty of fat to insulate him from the cold. Their boat hit the rocks near the harbor and broke up. They were all in the water, and Larson saw his friends getting dashed on the rocks, so he turned around and swam the other way. He headed for the first buoy, but it was a can buoy, a steel flotation drum about 6' X 10' with nothing to hold on to. He couldn't grip it anywhere; it was too big around, and too high above the water, so he kept going and swam out to the bell buoy. It had a metal structure to climb up on, and he rode it until some fishermen saw him in the morning and picked him up. He was the only survivor.

Sam's wife, Charlene, had put the children to bed about ten and tried to think positively. She discouraged her family from calling her to keep the phone line open. She prayed, cried, read a little for distraction. Finally she decided to lie down and at least try to get some rest, and she fell asleep.

About 2:30 a.m. the Coast Guard tried to telephone her to tell her they had found her husband alive. She was awakened by the ringing phone, but before she could answer it she smelled smoke and discovered that the house was in flames. The heater was on, and something too close to it must have caught on fire. She ran to the childrens' room, grabbed them both, and carried them outside. Within a few minutes, the whole house was a conflagration. She didn't find out for a couple of hours that Sam had been found.

When they finally got together, at her mother's house, Sam learned that the one tragedy had saved his family from the other. Charlene was so relieved that Sam was alive, she didn't even care that her home had burned to the ground. Neither one of them drew any conclusions about any portents for his fishing career. Sam was devastated by Louie's death; but at this time he didn't get any signals about giving up fishing. That freak wave could have happened to anybody.

Sam never talked about it, and his friends avoided raising the subject around him because he was so affected by the loss of his crewman. Sam had always been even-tempered. I wasn't around him a lot, but I never heard of him getting angry at anyone. Then one day a representative from the raft company came to Noyo to look him up, about three months after his boat capsized. Word had reached them that their raft had saved his life, and the company was hoping to get an endorsement for their product.

The representative was even more enthusiastic after he saw Sam; he would be perfect for a TV commercial promoting their brand of life-saving equipment. Their conversation was highly charged, but brief. Sam finally had somebody in front of him who deserved the blame for the one outcome that most distressed him, and they had the audacity to expect praise. A couple of Sam's friends were there, and they noticed Sam's muscles tighten. They were apprehensive about what he might do to the polite, crisply dressed sales rep, who was a much less dynamic personage than Sam's six feet of brawn. Sam took a minute to compose himself. Then, in a low, steady voice, he told the raft company representative never to come near him again, and to tell his company not to send anyone to see him, or call him, ever again. "If that sonofabitch had worked the way it was supposed to, my crewman would still be alive." The man sensed the danger, and left so fast he seemed to vanish; there was no further contact.

Sam's boat was insured, so he arranged to have a new boat built. The new boat had been in the water one week when he had his next devastating message from the deep.

They were crab fishing off Usal, near Shelter Cove, about 60 miles north of Noyo as the crow flies, or as the boat rolls; it's a lot farther by car, especially over the last 30 miles of winding dirt road. The weather was fair and the sea was a little choppy but not bad. You get white caps at 12 knots, so the wind was less than that. They had just pulled up the crab pots, and were getting ready to go home. There were three of them on board, and Sam was in the cabin at the wheel. The two crew members were in the stern stacking and securing the gear. They were in shallow water about a quarter mile from shore.

Sam started the engine and began to go forward at about half throttle, when something seemed to grab the back of the boat from under the surface. Sam heard a big "clunk". The stern started going under, and the two crewmen, who were standing near the transom, jumped off. Sam looked back and saw half the stern go under, so he thought maybe the new boat had split a seam, or something broke apart.

He went to full throttle, thinking if he got enough speed maybe he could spin the boat around and beach it. As he tried to accelerate, the whole stern went under, and water started to fill the cabin. Before he even had time to think of doing anything else, the cabin pressure became strong enough to blow the cabin window out, and Sam was blown out with it. Within 10 or 15 seconds, the whole boat was gone, and Sam was in the water. When he got over being dazed, there was no sign of where the boat had been, and no sign of the crewmen.

Despite his shock and astonishment, Sam's survival instincts took over. Sam knew the beach at Usal. Though it was remote, and a long way to go from Fort Bragg for beach fishing, it was one of the few beaches on the coast where you could catch the small smelt or grunion known as "night fish." These very small smelt that locals enjoy only run on beaches with a coarse type of sand. There are only three that I know of: Cleone, Juan Creek, and Usal.

The fish are similar to the smelt locals call "surf fish", but they are only about two inches long instead of four, and run in the surf only at night. They're so small, you don't even have to clean them. You eat them whole (except the heads), fresh fried or smoked. You have to get wet to catch them. You can't stay in the cold water for long without a break to get warm by a fire. Some people fish in wet suits or waders, but most locals fish in their jeans and bring an extra pair to change into. They use a V-shaped net about 4 feet long (just net on a home-made frame) and dip the wide end in the breaking surf, and then dump the fish in a wash tub or a wooden crate. It's a good excuse for a beach party or family campout.

You never knew when surf fish would be running, but all summer somebody is always trying. When they start catching anything, word gets around amazingly fast, and soon the closer beaches are mobbed with campers, kids, and dogs. Usal is too far from town, so it's never crowded unless you brought your own crowd. It's so remote here, the sea lions aren't even afraid of you. They come right up on the beach, and romp in the surf with the people fishing. It's the people who try to keep some distance. When surf fish have been running regularly, then you can usually catch night fish at the same beaches. Sam had been night fishing here as a child.

There were rocks north of it, but Sam knew where the beach was, and he headed south. It was a long swim, and when he got near the beach he was trying to body surf on the breakers to come in. He remembered when he did this as a kid. We didn't call it "body surfing"--it was just playing in the ocean. We waded out as far as we could, and jumped high when a big wave came. It would go by, and we could stand up until the next one came. When the waves got too big, we would turn around and try to ride one to shore. We never worried about sharks. I guess we thought they wouldn't try to hang around in the shallow, unpredictable surf when they had the whole ocean. We were in bathing suits, not in shiny black wetsuits dressed like their favorite food; we might have worried if they could mistake us for sea lions.

Sam had never tried this farther out than he could wade from the beach, and hadn't done it since high school, but his familiarity with the ocean guided him. It was easier to stay afloat and make some progress in the rough surf if you caught a wave and cooperated with it. He just hoped one wouldn't break and churn him around too long in the froth and bubbles. That happened to him a few times in his youth. About the time he was ready to give up and drown, the wave slapped him down on the beach and then retreated, leaving him on the cold sand in the foam. He was having a deja vu experience of this when he opened his eyes and realized it was cold reality.

Because he knew the beach, he also knew there was nothing at Usal but a couple of abandoned old cabins just beyond the water line from the beach that people sometimes camped in during the summer. There was a big sheep ranch that had a ranch house near the cove, but the owners didn't live there. Usually no one was around except for a few weeks in the summer.

This area is often called "the lost coast" or "the forgotten coast" because it's so inaccessible by car. It's the longest roadless section of the Pacific shoreline, except in Alaska. There was a mill at Usal in 1889 that closed in 1902 and then was destroyed by fire. Even then, there was only a primitive dirt road, the same one that still connects Usal to the outside world. The lumber was hauled out by the "doghole schooners" which by then were steam powered, and were loaded from wire chutes that extended out beyond the rocky cliffs.

Despite its isolation and insignificance today, Usal has its place in history as the origin of Dollar Steamship Lines. Captain Robert Dollar bought the Usal mill and property in 1894. Usal was one of the most treacherous of the "doghole ports", and shipping companies were reluctant to send their vessels there, so Captain Dollar had his first schooner built to his order in 1888. He went on to acquire his own fleet.

Sam knew he was a long way from civilization. At this point he wasn't really thinking, he was still functioning in shock and amazement, and maybe even some delirium. He knew on some level that new boats don't disappear without an explanation in fifteen seconds or less. He tried to think what had happened, but it was incomprehensible. He couldn't find any theory to entertain that didn't make him feel like he was losing his mind, so he just walked. He looked around the cabins, but there was no water. So he started walking up the road. He wished he had some shoes.

Sam had to walk for a day and a half before he found a house where someone was there. His feet were still in pretty good shape, again thanks to his childhood. Beach kids learn how to walk on rocks and gravel and watch out for broken glass. He startled the elderly couple, who had no warning of his approach from the sound of any vehicle, by his sudden desperate appearance and remarkable story. They didn't have a phone, but they gave him food and water and drove him into Westport in their muddy Dodge pickup. There was nothing there but a little bar and store in the old Westport Hotel, but they had a phone. He called Charlene to come and get him. There was a search, but his crewmen were never found.

Sam didn't weigh his options this time. He didn't consider getting another boat, even though his new boat was fully insured. The only thing he said to me, or any of his friends I talked to, was that something didn't want him to fish. He didn't know what he would do, but he was going to do something else.

The insurance company sent divers to investigate what happened to Sam's boat. It was a simple explanation. Not a sea monster, or at least not the type you might envision. The sea is incredibly powerful, sometimes powerful enough to pick up a heavily anchored buoy and carry it completely off course. Buoys are moored with stout chain to iron or concrete sinkers or clumps that weigh about six tons, depending on the nature of the sea bed. Normally they are found, but if they move far enough they may not be. Then they are just replaced. Buoy depth is 26 fathoms, and this particular buoy had been carried almost all the way into Shelter Cove into water about five fathoms deep.

The sunken old buoy was positioned so that the chain was under the surface, but high enough that it hit the propeller of Sam's boat. They found the boat with the chain wrapped around the propeller shaft, and that is what pulled the boat under. The more Sam accelerated, the faster it disappeared--mechanically assisted.

The insurance company thought about raising the boat, since it was new, but decided it would cost more to salvage it than it was worth. It was a relief to Sam to have an explanation for that bizarre experience, but it didn't reassure him to know that what happened to him was something you would never expect and could never anticipate. The unlikely odds of its happening only strengthened his conviction that his occupation as a fisherman was just not meant to be.

It would make sense if something in the universe didn't want me to fish. I got into it through sheer determination, not helped by heritage. But Sam was born into a fishing family, and he never did anything but fish. He had all the skills and aptitude for it, and he was good at it. Nobody was a better skipper or worked harder than Sam, and nobody had such bad luck with boats. If Sam can't depend on fishing for a living, I'm starting to wonder if anybody can. There's a lot that's outside your control.

I felt bad to see Sam quit. Maybe if I had ended up in the water three times, through no fault of my own, I might have reacted the same way. I couldn't help making comparisons with Alex Johnson, who kept losing boats and crewmen through his own incompetence, and didn't have the sense to quit. I would never get on another boat with Alex, though I wouldn't hesitate to go out on Sam's boat with him tomorrow and take my chances with fate. I'm not much inclined to believe in fate--free will is too important to me--but in this case I guess I'm ready to believe that fate might have intended Sam for better things.

CHAPTER 10

RECKONING

1976
Reckoning

Another day on the briny deep. There's high fog, and we're thankful for that because it tones down the blinding glare of the water on a clear day. There's no relief from the brightness until sundown, so we're always squinting. There's a pretty good chop, and the sensation on deck is like riding a bucking bronco bareback. We're standing on the stern sorting fish. We don't have much trouble with our footing. You never know what it will do, but you get a feel for it. You don't ever get really comfortable with it, but you like it anyway. But it's not for everybody. You have to be able to live with uncertainty. This is becoming a problem for me, for the first time.

The Big Dipper is still spending too much time out, and keeping me away from home. We're out almost all the time. It's not as much fun as trolling, and it's getting harder to take, now that we have Brian. I don't get to see him much. I'm doing some soul-searching about whether to keep fishing.

It's not so simple as just going back to trolling, which I'd like to do, because the industry has changed so much. When I started fishing in the sixties, salmon and albacore were booming. Nobody even bothered with bottom fish unless they were exceptionally good at trawling. If you have silver and gold, you don't go prospecting for iron. But now that's changed.

There's a lot of concern about depleting the salmon stocks, and salmon fishing is getting more restricted all the time. It seems like they close the season whenever the fish are here, and open it again when they're gone.

The big steel trawlers dominate the industry now, and the ones 80 feet or under dominate Noyo Harbor. Nothing much bigger than that can get in. Ten years ago there was hardly any market for bottom fish. Now there's a big frozen food market, and everybody in Iowa has fish sticks in their freezer. For the first time I'm starting to look at fishing as a career instead of a job, and it isn't looking encouraging for the kind of fishing I like to do.

There are still fishermen making a living on small boats the way they always did, but I need to look at how long that can last. There are also more boats for sale than usual, and they are not selling. If I had my own Makela brothers boat, I'd just keep doing it. But if it's unlikely I could ever do well enough to get one, maybe I should think about something else.

I don't make any snap decision, but I've been talking it over with some of my friends. One of them, Bill, has been in the Coast Guard for over ten years. He says he likes his job because every day is different in one way or another. He worked in a sawmill before that, first running an edger, then running a joiner, and than a rip saw. He said the only variety in any of those jobs, ever, was the length of the board. I can relate to that. In fact, it makes me wonder how many of us here are fishing for just that reason.

In the 60s you could have described Fort Bragg as a lumber town, but that would have been an understatement.

Life in the community was regulated by the blast of a mill whistle. The mayor's regular job was public relations for the Union Lumber Company. Whatever the company wanted to do was pretty much okay with most of the folks who lived here. The company employed the majority of them, and took pretty good care of them. They could charge anything they needed at the company store: groceries, clothes, furniture and even appliances.

Some of the fishermen lived in Fort Bragg, and some in Mendocino, but they didn't care much what happened in Fort Bragg. The company had no influence over their lives; their interests were centered on their boats at Noyo.

The thing we all had in common was we all made our living from the natural resources of the area. The thing that was vastly different was the insulating role the company played between the mill workers and their resource. Loggers had closer contact working in the forests, but they were still far removed from harvesting the trees themselves, and building something with them or selling them. The fishermen have that direct role.

Because of that, the fishermen have an autonomy that very few professions offer. We don't have a benevolent guardian of our livelihood; we have to connive and trick it out of rocks and shoals and currents. But what we do is direct and personal, between us and the ocean. When we sell the fish, we have to deal in the same commercial realm as the millworkers, but most of the time we're free of it. We can make all of our own decisions. I think this appeals to me as much as the excitement.

We say this is our livelihood, but it's much more than that: it's our vitality. You feel like every minute counts. The physical work you do is an expression of your spirit, like being in the Olympics every day with no audience but yourself. The fishermen here are not in it for the money, or they would get out of it, because the money is not that regular. Most of them are attracted to fishing because of a lifelong connection to the ocean, like I am.

I've heard people speculate about the small boat fisherman's "relationship with the ocean." If someone asked me about that, I'd tell them he can reach it from the gaff hatch. It can splash him when it kicks up. He tastes the salt on his lips and smells it in the air. The ocean is right there, a few feet away, in its deep, green, unfathomable splendor. He sees sharks and sea lions when he looks down the side of the boat, and kelp and whatever else is swimming or floating around him. It's not an abstraction.

Seven-tenths of the earth's surface is water. I'd feel like I was really limiting myself if my life were restricted to the land.

Now I've tried every kind of fishing except crabbing, which I decided a long time ago to avoid. I have enough experience to feel confident with my own boat. It's time to start in that direction, if I'm ever going to, or to think about doing something else. It's decision time.

A skipper I like and respect just offered me a job on a Makela brothers boat. He has been fishing with an older brother on the family boat. His brother is retiring, and he's close to retiring himself. There's no one else to take over the boat, and he has mentioned some arrangement for me to buy it over time. Nothing specific; he just wants me to know that it's a possibility.

This is what I've always wanted. Now it's time for me to find out if it's really what I'll choose, taking other people into account. And for figuring out if I have to. I guess I know the answer to that. But to quit fishing seems about as simple to me as for a planet to change its orbit.

I have to make a tough choice, and when I do that kind of thinking I always go to the ocean. I drive up Highway One north and turn off at the road to Cleone Beach. I walk out on the ocean bluff. It's brisk and clear and the surf is high. It's blowin', as Rudy would say.

I thought I'd never give up fishing. Now there are some other things I want in my life that I know I'll never have if I don't give it up. I'm also considering the implications for my wife and family if I do, or if I don't. What are the possibilities for them?

I've been thinking about that comment my friend made so long ago, that fishermen are very selfish with their lives. I have to admit that's true. It's true even of the ones that do it because it's what they have always done, and probably don't have as much fun at it as I do. None of us shares much of it with anyone, and it doesn't leave much time for sharing anything else either. There's no question that I'm doing it for myself. I'd never give it up if I were the only one to consider now.

I watch the blustery whitecaps, and the wind blowing the frothy tops of the breakers into spray, thinking about the ocean's mood extremes, its reactions to the wind, and to unseen forces and distant changing weather. Looking north I can see unending rows of waves swelling, rising and breaking along the miles of beach. I watch the breakers roll in relentlessly...eternally. I begin to feel better. It will still be there when I'm ready to go fishing again.

I'm giving it up for a family life that will be more gratifying in the long term than a thrill every day. I'll just have to get my excitement from recreation the way normal people do. It's not such a big sacrifice, except that Vi and I will both be leaving home to move inland. I don't have that many options for earning a living here, and I know I would always go back to fishing if we stay on the coast.

The Mendocino Coast is spectacular, and growing up here makes you take natural beauty for granted. Most young people here move away for better job opportunities, but not because they want to. Vi and I both had idyllic childhoods of playing on white sandy beaches, and romping in the surf.

Behind the school there was a redwood forest with a creek and fallen logs and hollowed redwood forts, with salamanders and banana slugs, and an occasional little harmless snake. We all played there as children in a woodland only rarely visited by grown-ups, a fantasy world of our own.

On weekends we would picnic with our families in other redwood forests dripping with fog, with rays of sunlight streaming through the trees. Pink rhododendrons and lush ferns grew among them, with wild ladyslipper orchids and the rare salmon berries we could eat that looked like pale golden raspberries and tasted like--well, like water, but slightly sweet. There were huckleberries, but I never liked those. They're little blueberries, mostly skin, that always seemed to me to taste like it must taste eating ants. And there were stinging nettles in the woods that looked a lot like the salmon berry bushes. If you reminisce long enough, you start thinking of things that make you realize maybe everything isn't so idyllic after all.

As childhoods go, though, we were so fortunate. From my house we could walk to the beaches, climb down paths on the rocky cliffs covered with wild purple iris, and find seashells on the beach or make forts with the driftwood. It's going to be hard for us to leave all this. We can always come back to visit like so many of our friends do.

1976-1998

Vi and I move to Greenville in rural Plumas County, and discover the beauty of mountain lakes and streams. I learn to sail on lakes, and Vi and our two sons get to be competent sailors. We move near Susanville in rural Lassen County, and discover the natural beauty of the high desert. I learn that my grandfather was born five miles down the road from our home, and lived here most of his life, so these are my roots after all--far from the ocean.

I'm a corrections officer at the state prison, so my job isn't dull. I'm content to defer the ocean excitement for now, but I haven't given up my dreams. I'd like to sail the Transpac race from San Francisco to Hawaii someday. I have an Olson 30 that won it twice. I'll have to wait until

I get some time to train in the ocean, but the day will come. Sailboat racing is not that different from the rewards of fishing: you risk your life, and if you win, you might get a silver pickle dish. But it's harder to justify, because you don't earn the money to do it by selling fish.

I still think about fishing every day.

1999
Noyo Harbor at the Turn of the Century

Fishing has changed so much, it's an entirely different experience today than it was in the 60s and 70s. The most dramatic change is satellite navigation. All the boats have global positioning satellite equipment that tells them precisely where they are on the globe every minute. There are even small hand-held units, so everybody has one. There's no need to bother with Loran, or ever have to guess.

For me there's a high that goes with being out on the Pacific--in 67 million square miles of ocean--and not knowing exactly where. Knowing where that little pinpoint is might not change anything physically, but psychologically it changes everything. That takes a lot of the wonder out of it for me. Today's fishermen will never experience the feeling of being lost in such vastness. Unless their GPS fails--and then God help them.

The twentieth century brought amazing advances in navigation safety, and the twenty-first is saying goodbye to them just as fast. Dots and dashes will be a thing of the past soon, and the telegraph will be replaced by e-mail. The International Marine Organization called for commercial ships to replace their radiotelegraph communications with a new technology called the Global Marine Distress and Safety System by February 1, 2000. Now, instead of tapping out SOS and having it relayed by a ship-to-shore station, ships can push one button to alert nearby ships of any specific problem--whether it's a fire, sinking, capsizing, or sitting dead in the water.

It's a terrible thought to me for fishermen to be out there with cell phones and e-mail. You might as well be a stock broker. Today nobody would even consider going out of sight of land with only the equipment we had. That's normal. As technology advances you think you couldn't live without whatever is standard for the day, but you don't miss what you never had. You manage with what you've got, and then--looking back--it seems like the dark ages, and you sound like an old timer describing it. But then, as now, it changed radically in a decade. Fishing is never the same experience it was ten years earlier, unless you're like Rudy.

If Rudy were still around, he'd probably be playing with last year's castoff GPS somebody gave him, just to see how it worked. If it was simple enough he might use it, but I'm sure he wouldn't ever be depending on it. Rudy survived everything the ocean dealt him, and was in his eighties when he died. He never was a highliner; just a master fisherman who believed that life was contest enough. He's going to be with me in spirit when I sail the Transpac singlehanded.

Killer Willie retired from fishing in his 40s and runs a very successful store in Fort Bragg. He probably doesn't do anything the way other retailers do it; and he probably still gives the impression that he's just having a good time and makes a fortune by accident.

Alex didn't ever get another boat after the St. Jude went on the rocks. He turned out to be a popular bartender. I would never have predicted that, but I guess it makes sense. He was pleasant to be around on land.

Ted recovered his loss the first year. A couple of years later he sold the Big Dipper and got a bigger boat, and kept up the pace for about five years. He sold it and retired a few years ago.

Nobody knows what happened to Ollie. He's not around anymore.

Joe Silveira retired, and his sons are still fishing out of Noyo with his Makela brothers boat, the Maria, and doing quite well.

Now some of my old friends make most of their income from crab. There are too many restrictions on salmon, and crab is highly competitive, so they take bigger risks than they used to. The crab is grabbed up by bigger boats that move into the area within a couple of weeks-- long before the season ends-- so the local boats have to go out in all kinds of weather while the crab is still there.

The rest of the time they catch fresh market fish like red snapper, sole, ling cod and halibut. It doesn't pay as well as salmon and albacore, but the small boats can afford to fish where the supply wouldn't support big commercial boats, and they can make a living.

Some fishing boats have been converted to party boats to take groups out on whale watching expeditions. Rudy and I used to get a little nervous when we got too close to whales. They are curious and can tip you over accidentally without meaning any harm. But I haven't heard of any boats capsizing on whale-watching trips.

Carl Youngdahl is a multi-millionaire in his sixties, and is still fishing. He sold his Makela brothers boat, and bought a 90-foot wooden boat, and fishes out of Humboldt Bay. Now he has a crew.

Sam is in charge of the scales for one of the fish dealers. He seems content, and he and Charlene spend a lot of time with their families. He has a new pickup.

The big steel boat that was being built next to the Big Dipper is rusty, and is still there. It never did get finished. Its owner died of old age. I don't know who owns it now, but it's nothing but a relic too big to dispose of. It's not going to sea.

Makela Boat Works is still at Noyo, and Fred Makela's son, Howard, is still repairing wooden boats, and building the finest wooden boats time, patience, master craftsmanship and money can buy. But instead of commercial fishing boats, the last two were a ketch-rigged 36-foot sailboat, and a 42-foot schooner.

I'm in the high desert, remembering moments like the unforgettable spectacle of a misty sunrise on the still Pacific on a perfect day, or the pleasure of coming in the channel after a bonanza trip.

Several runs of Pacific Coast salmon are on the endangered species list. The fishermen on small wooden boats are too, but I wouldn't give up on them. They will be around as long as there's an ocean, because there will always be fishermen the world over who know what I know. We're too independent to have any cult or secret handshake, but if we did we would have a maxim, and keep it carefully guarded from the prying and curious. It would be something like this one that William Henry Davies wrote about a private passion:

> *I'll make my Joy a secret thing,*
> *My face shall wear a mask of care;*
> *And those who hunt a Joy to death,*
> *Shall never know what sport is there!*

ISBN 155212815-6